John Cornwell

EARTH
TO
EARTH

*A true story of the lives and violent
deaths of a Devon farming family*

PENGUIN BOOKS

FOR JOHN GUEST

Penguin Books Ltd, 27 Wrights Lane, London w8 5tz (Publishing and Editorial)
and Harmondsworth, Middlesex, England (Distribution and Warehouse)
Viking Penguin Inc., 40 West 23rd Street, New York, New York 10010, USA
Penguin Books Australia Ltd, Ringwood, Victoria, Australia
Penguin Books Canada Ltd, 2801 John Street, Markham, Ontario, Canada l3r 1b4
Penguin Books (NZ) Ltd, 182–190 Wairau Road, Auckland 10, New Zealand

First published by Allen Lane 1982
Published in Penguin Books 1984
Reprinted 1987

Copyright © John Cornwell, 1982
All rights reserved

Made and printed in Great Britain by
Richard Clay Ltd, Bungay, Suffolk
Set in Baskerville

PENGUIN BOOKS

EARTH TO EARTH

John Cornwell was born in London in 1940. He read English at Oxford, following this with research at Cambridge. He then worked as a freelance journalist mainly overseas until 1976 when he joined the staff of the *Observer*, where he is now editor of the newspaper's Foreign News Service.

He is the author of two novels – *The Spoiled Priest* and *Seven Other Demons* – and his last book was a biography of Samuel Taylor Coleridge. He is married with two children and lives in Northamptonshire.

John Cornwell won the Crime Writers' Association Gold Dagger Award for non-fiction with *Earth to Earth*.

Contents

List of Plates

The truth is, we are murdered by
our ancestors. Their dead hands stretch
forth from the tomb and drag us down.

RICHARD JEFFERIES,
The Story of My Heart

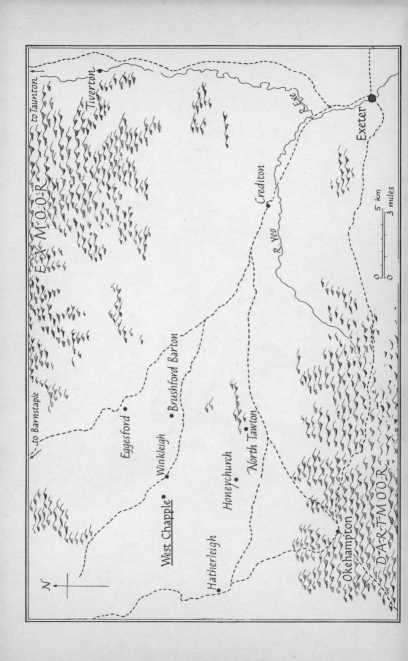

EXMOOR

to Taunton

Tiverton

to Barnstaple

Eggesford

Winkleigh

Brushford Barton

West Chapple

Hatherleigh

Honeychurch

North Tawton

Okehampton

DARTMOOR

Crediton

R. Yeo

Exe

Exeter

N

5 km
3 miles

0
0

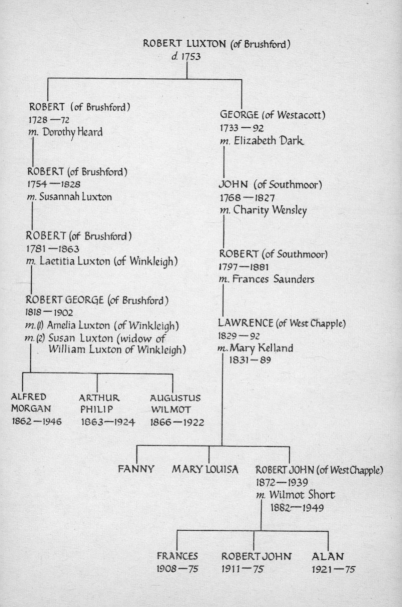

ROBERT LUXTON (of Brushford)
d. 1753

ROBERT (of Brushford)
1728—72
m. Dorothy Heard

ROBERT (of Brushford)
1754—1828
m. Susannah Luxton

ROBERT (of Brushford)
1781—1863
m. Laetitia Luxton (of Winkleigh)

ROBERT GEORGE (of Brushford)
1818—1902
m.(1) Amelia Luxton (of Winkleigh)
m.(2) Susan Luxton (widow of
        William Luxton of Winkleigh)

ALFRED   ARTHUR   AUGUSTUS
MORGAN   PHILIP   WILMOT
1862—1946   1863—1924   1866—1922

GEORGE (of Westacott)
1733—92
m. Elizabeth Dark

JOHN (of Southmoor)
1768—1827
m. Charity Wensley

ROBERT (of Southmoor)
1797—1881
m. Frances Saunders

LAWRENCE (of West Chapple)
1829—92
m. Mary Kelland
   1831—89

FANNY   MARY LOUISA   ROBERT JOHN (of West Chapple)
1872—1939
m. Wilmot Short
   1882—1949

FRANCES   ROBERT JOHN   ALAN
1908—75   1911—75   1921—75

In Pursuit of the Luxtons

It all began with a newspaper article sent through the post to my home with FYI scrawled in the margin. There was no date on the cutting, but it was the last week in September and the story was peculiarly apt for an English autumn.

The piece was headlined: 'Tragic Farm Where Time Stood Still'. It was written by Pearson Phillips in the *Observer* and it began: 'Alongside the farming notes and the recipes for windfall apples, the local newspapers of Devon and Cornwall have been aghast all week at a stark tragedy.'

The tragedy concerned three members of a farming family, the Luxtons, who had been found slaughtered in strange circumstances at West Chapple Farm near Winkleigh in Mid-Devon. There was mention of 'blasted bodies', disappointed love affairs, wrangles over property, and all against the background of a remote farm that had somehow managed to escape the progress of the twentieth century.

'The story which emerges has a unique and chilling fascination,' wrote Phillips. In fact, I found the story so fascinating that I immediately set off for the Press Association Library in Fleet Street to see if I could discover more on the newspaper files.

Coverage of the Winkleigh killings, which had occurred four days previously, was extensive. There were reports in *The Times*, the *Daily Telegraph* and the *Daily Mail*. The West Country press was full of it, especially the *Express and Echo*: 'Night of Horror at Winkleigh' proclaimed the front page. Sitting in the library I made a summary of all the accounts.

*

On the previous Wednesday morning a grocer's rounds-man, Jimmy Reynolds, had called at an isolated farm near Winkleigh called West Chapple, which had been owned and run since before the war by two brothers, Robbie and Alan Luxton, and their eldest sister, Frances. She was aged 68, Robbie 65, and Alan 53. All three had been born on the farm, as had their father before them; none of them had married.

When Reynolds arrived in the farmyard he saw what he thought was a white scarecrow lying on an incline next to a barn. The place was deserted and a dog was barking in an outhouse.

'I couldn't take my eyes off the scarecrow thing. It looked so strange and it was attracting a lot of attention from the flies,' he told the police. 'I backed the van up watching it all the time.'

He approached the farmhouse door and knocked, but there was no answer. Then he walked slowly across the yard to examine the 'scarecrow'. To his horror he found Alan Luxton's body, dressed in pyjamas and unlaced army boots. The body was lying, arms folded, in a pool of dark blood. The scalp was completely missing from below the eyes. Reynolds poked the arm with a stick and found that it was still supple. There was no weapon to be seen.

He raced back to Winkleigh and reported what he had seen to the police. Within an hour a full-scale investigation had been set up under a CID man called Detective Chief Super-intendent Proven Sharpe. Forensic experts were flown in by helicopter from Bristol.

It was feared that a killer might still be lurking, so the police (in constabulary parlance) 'proceeded with caution', calling out as they went. Fragments of flesh and bone and pieces of brain were found over a wide area around the farmhouse: on the lawn and in the flower-beds at the back of the house, by the farm gate, and at the entrance to the orchard.

The police had to break into the house, which had apparently been locked from the inside; but the dead man's brother and sister were nowhere to be found.

Creeping through the vegetable garden by the orchard fence Police Constable Tilke at last came upon their corpses lying side by side in the grass among rotting cider apples. They had been hidden from view by a fold in the earth. Frances had her nightgown up around her midriff; she was lying in an eerie posture, on all fours, her legs drawn up as if in prayer. The top of her head was missing and a large section of brain, apparently intact, lay several feet from her body as if it had just flopped out. Alongside was the body of her brother Robbie, dressed in trousers, unlaced boots and a vest. He too had massive head injuries and, in addition, several cuts right through the cheek and about the lips, mouth and ears. An old shotgun lay at his side.

The bodies were removed to a mortuary at Exeter where they were later identified by Fred Lyne, the Luxtons' farm labourer. Lyne had stood in a meadow watching as Reynolds sped down the track on his way to report to the police, but he claimed to have been unaware that anything was amiss.

The circumstances of the family's deaths had 'all the marks of an Agatha Christie thriller', said the police constable at Winkleigh with relish. The background details, however, seemed to me even more irresistible. The 'deceased trio', as the Press liked to call them, were the last surviving members of an ancient Devon farming family that had been settled at West Chapple since at least the fourteenth century. They were recluses: the youngest brother, Alan, it was claimed, had not been seen beyond the farm gate for twenty years. In recent years little had been seen of the other two; only on rare occasions had they emerged together in Winkleigh – weather-beaten, and emaciated as skeletons.

They had farmed their 230 acres in the same manner and

with the same equipment as their grandfather had in the mid
nineteenth century. While concrete had appeared on most
farms even in this secluded part of Devon, the yards and cow-
sheds of West Chapple Farm were paved with centuries-old
cobbles; the great barns were supported by medieval beams.
The meadows were mown with scythes and the hay turned
and rowed and stacked with pitchforks. Post-and-wire fences
were unknown; every hedge had been cut and layered to
perfection by time-honoured methods.

They had lived and worked without mains electricity and
water. Energy was generated in a wooden shed next to the
house. Inside stood a great iron water-wheel sunk deep into
the ground. The wheel was fed by wooden culverts from a
pond above the farm and linked by a system of gears and
jointed shafts to perfectly maintained Victorian machinery
in a barn on the slope above the house. The rain squalls sweep-
ing across the moors from the Atlantic provided free power.

'We are not clear as to who did what to whom and in what
sequence,' said Proven Sharpe at a press conference. 'We are
treating the case as a murder inquiry, but at the moment we
are holding an open mind as to what occurred. Our investigations are centred on the farm and the immediate area of Winkleigh, and we do not anticipate at this stage that we shall
extend them further.'

All the same, interviews with local people had stimulated
a proliferation of rumours and theories: suicide pact, a com-
bination of suicide and murder, a beserk psychopath . . .

Reading through the various newspaper accounts, I real-
ized that the majority of the journalists had found the story
attractive because the killings had occurred in a rural setting,
where people are supposed to be healthy, content and safe.
Some, however, had been intrigued by the Luxtons' resistance
to progress, and had written their stories from a rather different perspective: here was a family apparently enjoying the

authentic, rustic existence of their nineteenth-century forebears, pursuing the ideal of 'self-sufficiency' untainted by
mechanization and chemical fertilizers; and yet the idyll had
ended in nightmare. Was it the intrusion of progress that had
led to their deaths? Or had their lives in fact been less than
idyllic?

The newspaper reports had stirred my imagination and
deeply stimulated my curiosity, but I knew that the journalists,
the police and even the Coroner's Court were unlikely to
provide satisfying answers to the questions raised by these
strange events.

The next day I drove from London down to Winkleigh,
which lies in a stretch of ancient farmland between Exmoor
and Dartmoor known as Mid-Devon. The September sky was
soft blue and contrasted strongly with the bright moss green
of the pastureland. The soil in this part of Devon is dark cedar-
red; it is a pervasive hue in the landscape and blends with
the red sandstone and cob from which so many local barns
and homesteads are built. The country here is secretive, with
abrupt combes screened by sturdy coppices. Great Saxon
earth banks topped by layered thickets border the weirdly
patterned fields and lanes, and the lush meadows lie in soft
folds, shaped by ancient warrens and cattle-ways. Sheltered,
yet drenched by pure water, the soil is wonderfully fertile.
The land is good for beef-fattening, sheep-raising and dairy
farming. In addition most farmers tend orchards and keep
pigs and poultry.

Along the Exeter to Barnstaple road the names of the
parishes and 'hundreds' bear witness to the antiquity of the
communities: Frithlestock, Buckland Brewer, Woolfardis-
worthy, Clovella Dykes, Zeal Monachorum, Cruwys Mor-
chard.

Cut off by their hidden combes and valleys, and their traditional reserve towards all outsiders, the inhabitants are thrown on to their own resources. In this part of Devon the lanes are frequently impassable for days, sometimes for weeks in a bad winter. In summer men and women often work outside from dawn till bedtime. Kinship and acquaintance are close-knit.

Winkleigh, with its pinnacled church tower of All Saints, stands on the summit of a hill looking out towards the blue haze of the moors – Dartmoor to the south and Exmoor to the north. My guide book told me that the village had been founded in the days of the Saxon occupation of Devon. At some unknown date it had acquired a fair and a market, growing to a height of prosperity from which it had slipped into decline with the coming of the railway, which had by-passed Winkleigh and favoured Eggesford. Nowadays Winkleigh's population is little more than half what it was in the early nineteenth century.

I went inside the church and found it spacious and light; the roof beams and bosses are gaily painted and there is a huge and ornate oak screen. Outside I found some truly grotesque dog-head gargoyles and a sun-dial with this grim reminder:

> Life's but a show, Man's but dust
> This dyall says, Dy all we must.

The churchyard stands open to the blustery winds high above the village and looks out over Winkleigh's huddle of cob and rough-cast dwellings across rolling hills to Brushford Barton and Coldridge. Wandering among the graves I noted the recurring names on the headstones: Chambers, Saunders, Colihole, Knapman, Kennard, Tadbold, and, above all, Luxton.

Passing through the lych-gate, I walked down a narrow, deserted street to the village square. There was one monument, a neglected pyramid-shaped pump built to commemorate the passing of the Reform Bill in the reign of William IV. On the back it said simply: 'Erected by the Lord of the Manor 1832'.

Beyond it was Winkleigh's single concession to the twentieth century – the Crafty Bun Café. A scowling youth in dark glasses and combat jacket leaned against the doorway. He wore a tropical army hat with a badge saying: 'If you feel sexy – smile.' He had various Nazi insignia on his jacket and wore an earring.

I asked him if he lived in Winkleigh.

Looking straight ahead, and blushing deeply, he mumbled: 'Maybe, maybe not.' To my amazement Winkleigh's cafeteria cowboy was speechless with shyness.

Did he know how to get to West Chapple Farm?

He shook his head and pointed up the square to the pub: 'You wanna ask up there.' Then he turned back into the Crafty Bun where a group of youths in studded leather jackets sat around a greasy table. There was an atmosphere of over-brewed tea and stale cakes. A juke box thumped out a Heavy Metal number.

One of them asked if I was a journalist. I said that I was house-hunting. I asked what they did for a living and they told me they worked at the chicken factory beyond the disused airfield. 'Ah, yeah, thass just near them Luxtons,' said one.

They said that they slaughtered chickens. One of them giggled darkly; he wore a denim waistcoat but no shirt. His arms were covered in lurid tattoos. On the fingers of his right hand he had tattooed L-O-V-E, and on the fingers of the left, H-A-T-E. 'We grab 'em and hang 'em upside down on the merry-go-round. They don' 'alf squawk. Then chop, chop, CHOP – blood everywhere.'

What did they think of Winkleigh?

'Dead! Nothin' doin',' said one. 'No wonder people get topped.'

'You think the Luxtons were topped?'

'Course.'

'But why?'

'Serves 'em right for keeping it all under the bed.'

The King's Arms Hotel was the sort of village pub that had captured a corner of the county restaurant trade. There were fancy quiches and pâtés and cold meats on offer for lunch and an extensive dinner menu. There were scrubbed deal tables and intimate dining booths.

Two men stood at the bar in silence: one was middle-aged, a local farmworker by his clothes. The younger man was dressed in a tweed suit.

I bought a glass of beer and asked them if they could tell me the way to West Chapple Farm.

The older man immediately came to the point: 'You're going the right way to get a boot in yer face,' he murmured softly. Then he drank up and walked out.

The younger man grinned amicably and said: 'Never mind him. It was the journalists – they trampled over people's feelings. You've never seen anything like it. Great droves of them scrambling about all over the place, knocking on doors, asking stupid questions. Then they go away and write something completely different. Make it all up. You're not a journalist are you?'

I told him that I might be interested in buying the house. Then he said that he was a travelling salesman for a fertilizer company and lived in Hatherleigh. He spent his life travelling around Mid-Devon and knew almost everybody when it came to farming, but he did not know the Luxtons: 'They had no call for that sort of thing,' he chuckled. But he knew of one person in the village who might know about the property –

Clifford Short, a distant cousin of the Luxtons. Then there was Fred Lyne who had been the farm labourer at West Chapple for twenty-five years.

'That's your old-fashioned Devon farmer for you,' said the young man. 'You know, they gave Lyne a week's notice after all those years *and* expected him to work it out. Not a penny compensation ... nothing! Fred's working down at Inch's cider factory now. Stopped working one day for the Luxtons and started up the next at Inch's.'

'Has Lyne been a suspect?'

'God no! Old Fred wouldn't hurt a fly.'

I walked down the hill and out of Winkleigh on the Exeter road. The wind had dropped and the sun shed a rich early evening light; the leaves were turning on a line of fine oaks in the fields ahead. Elm Tree Cottage had massive white-washed walls and a thatched roof. Mrs Short was bent over a flower-bed in her garden, dead-heading roses that had been killed in the previous night's frost.

She was a squarish woman in an apron and her grey hair was held neatly in a hairnet. She wore heavy horn-rimmed spectacles. She seemed nervous and rather vague. Her husband was out working, but she was keen to talk about the Luxtons. She asked me almost hopefully if I was a detective.

'Why don't you come in for some tea,' she said.

Inside the cottage every effort had been made to eliminate the old rusticity; the room was filled with the bright textures and patterns of the high-street department store. A paraffin heater warmed the sitting room. She brought in a tray of tea and biscuits and settled by the window, where she twitched back the nylon lace curtain every time a car passed on the road.

'My husband wouldn't let me say anything if he were here. He was related to their mother, Wilmot. I'm no relative at all to the deceased. But you see, I think people ought to know about these things. I think one should have it out so as to avoid unhappiness. All this bottling things up never did any good.

'The Luxtons were completely shut up in themselves in recent years. The entrance to the farm is only three or four mile up the road, but I haven't set foot inside there for over forty years. The last time I was in there was just before the war when I went to the old father's funeral – that's their father. Mind you, I can't get about as much as I'd like. There's only the van, and my husband has that.

'The Luxtons were rather stuck up in a way, well-spoken. They had no truck with the likes of us. There was no television or anything like that, but she went abroad once, I think to the Holy Land. She was very religious and quite a reader. She was very keen on church. It was quite a joke around here, her going to the Holy Land, because they never had any money. At least they never spent any money. She's even been known to ask for one shoe-lace at the village shop; went into the shop and asked if they could separate a pair of laces because she was too mean to buy the whole pair. They had no time for the village, and as far as I know they had no friends. We're their closest relations – second or third cousins, I think – but they had nothing to do with us. Now everybody wants to know what's going to happen about the property. Well, it's all a mystery, all in a mess. A Mr Cloke over in Okehampton is the solicitor. The solicitor's working it all out. I don't suppose there will be anything for us. But just think what a house and 200 acres would fetch on the market now. It was under offer I think when they died.'

Mrs Short gave me the names of some people who might like to talk and told me about the funeral of Frances Luxton, which was to be held at Brushford Barton the next day.

'The brothers were cremated and buried today at Wink-leigh, but Frances is to be laid to rest over at Brushford. She

was always up there, moping about in the graveyard. I don't
know what she was doing I'm sure. But I don't know why
they're being buried separately like that.'

As I left Mrs Short's garden I looked back and saw the
curtains twitch at the darkening window.

I stayed on a farm near Winkleigh that did bed, breakfast
and evening meal. Four times I missed the entrance to the
farm as I got more and more confused in the deep and tortuous
lanes. The night was palpably black as I finally edged down
the mile-long drive to Headlands Manor Farm. The headlights
lit up a thick tunnel of trees. Eventually a rusting wreck of
an abandoned car came into view, then a collapsed hayrick.
The eerie shape of some outgrown topiary was silhouetted
against the ivied ruins of a cob barn.

At last there was a stone gateway surmounted by stone orbs,
and an oil lamp glimmered in a window ahead. In the farmyard at the back there was rusting machinery and sheep
nibbled at the rampant couch-grass and spreading bindweed.
A dog barked inside the house and a man appeared at the
door, cursing the dog and greeting me at the same time. He
shook my hand with an excruciating grip. As I entered the
kitchen I was shocked to find another man almost identical
to the one who had welcomed me. These were the bachelor
Heath brothers, who had farmed Headlands for thirty years.
They were tall with neat monkish haircuts and the quiet
studied manners of off-duty Jesuits. They wore ancient flannel
trousers and old cricket sweaters emblazoned with school or
house colours.

Derek, the elder by three or four years, was probably in
his late fifties. He did the cooking and most of the talking.
His silver hair was plastered down over the sides of his temples
in the manner of fifty years ago. Both brothers had been at
Stonyhurst College, the famous Jesuit school, during the war;

the one memory they had brought away with them was of being frequently flailed on the hands with a whale-bone covered in rubber. This was the Stonyhurst 'tolley'. 'Imagine if we'd been budding concert pianists,' said Derek. And both of them chortled in unison.

They smoked continuously as we waited for dinner, Derek delicately nursing the perilously small cigarette end in his enormous hands above the trifle he was preparing.

'Anyway,' he went on, 'I remember being beaten so badly at the end of term that the bruises were still there when I went back at the end of the holidays.'

On leaving Stonyhurst he had gone out to Canada to develop a 26,000-acre tract of forest and lakes as a sporting estate for tourists. 'After several winters alone in the Canadian backwoods I threw in the towel. All I left behind me was a few log cabins I built with my own hands.'

He had returned to England to 'open up' Headlands which had been owned by his father, and his younger brother had joined him to do the farming.

'Those early days were marvellous,' said Derek. 'Every morning I'd throw a tennis racket or my golf clubs into the back of my open Bentley and I'd be off all day in pursuit of pleasure. In the evening we'd play bridge.'

Over dinner the conversation turned to the Luxtons.

'I know a bloke who nearly sold a house to them,' said Derek. 'They put the farm on the market because they couldn't cope and they got interested in this little house over at Crediton. According to this chap, Frances Luxton turned up wearing white ankle socks and an old straw hat. And Robbie Luxton fell asleep on the sofa.

'They changed their minds about twenty times. Morning after morning he got a letter either confirming or cancelling the offer. Frances even called him in the night from a phone box. In the end he got fed up and told them to go to hell.'

On the way up the creaking oak staircase I passed various
dingy rooms filled to the ceiling with books. Everywhere was
that distinctive ammoniac smell of ancient rotting leather-
bound books. There were books in stacks on the gallery at
the top of the stairs, and great drifts of books in my bedroom.
I slept in a high old-fashioned bed at the front of the house.
The window was open on to the black starless night, and every
so often I awoke to the sound of rain and cattle scuffing below
the window.

It was still raining in the morning. I was lying in an oak-
panelled chamber with plaster crumbling from the Eliza-
bethan moulding on the high ceiling. I stood at the window
and looked out on an eighteenth-century pastoral landscape.
In the fields nearest the house were clumps of fine trees, oak,
beech, elm and chestnut, spreading proudly in their prime.
Cattle stood motionless in this parkland beneath a steady
curtain of rain. Beyond the fields flowed a brimming stream
smudged and faintly steamy in the downpour, and in the
further pastures the trees merged into the indistinct backdrop
of Dartmoor.

It was nine o'clock and the brothers were still in bed. I
made a cup of tea in the black and greasy recesses of the
ancient kitchen while their massive hound nosed me suspiciously. Then I went out to Frances Luxton's funeral.

On the lane back to the road the Heaths' farm appeared
to be in a remarkable state of ruin. The fine old hedges had
grown out completely and the banks were collapsing and
broken through in field after field. Whole tracts of coverts
were reverting to the appearance of virgin woodland, and the
animals wandered at will.

In Brushford churchyard the headstones leaned crazily this
way and that through sodden ferns and tufts of wild grass.

A line of dripping beech trees looked out over steep lush hill-side pastures. Carrion crows cursed high between the trees and the church tower.

The service was brief. The congregation numbered no more than twenty souls and I recognized only Mrs Short. Two large men eyed me carefully from the back; they were not dressed in mourning and had the unmistakable stamp of Devon and Cornwall CID all over them. Nobody wept. On the damp wall I noticed a memorial to 'Rev. John Luxton, 45 years, curate, died 1873'.

During the service an impressive-looking character with white hair went up into the Jacobean pulpit and read a passage from Ecclesiastes, which included the following lines in the King James version:

Remember now thy Creator in the days of thy youth, while the evil days come not, nor the years draw nigh, when thou shalt say, I have no pleasure in them; while the sun, or the light, or the moon, or the stars, be not darkened, nor the clouds return after the rain: in the day when the keepers of the house shall tremble, and the strong men shall bow themselves, and the grinders cease because they are few, and those that look out of the windows be darkened, and the doors shall be shut in the streets, when the sound of the grinding is low, and he shall rise up at the voice of the bird, and all the daughters of music shall be brought low.

At the back of the church I found the following entry in the visitors' book: 'Brian Luxton, B.A. If you have any information please contact.' There followed an address in Barry, Wales.

I hung about at the church door hoping for an opportunity to speak with someone. Mrs Short, who was with her husband, did not seem to recognize me, and the other mourners seemed to guess that I was a stranger and evaded my eye. The police-men scrutinized me carefully again and hurried off in the rain.

After the last car had gone I followed the track below the church and came out into a sweep-drive before a fine eighteenth-century manor-house with a grand portico surmounted by a wrought-iron balcony. The house looked out over open farmland towards Dartmoor.

Mrs Ennismore was a handsome, auburn-haired lady in her thirties whose husband made a living out of renovating and selling veteran cars. She was half-amused, half-frightened by the 'Winkleigh Killings', as all the locals and Press now called the Luxtons' deaths. She told me that her house had once belonged to Robert George Luxton, a notorious hunting squire who was a great-uncle of Frances and her brothers.

'I didn't know Frances,' she said, 'but I sometimes saw her sitting in the graveyard in the most incredibly old-fashioned clothes. Her family once owned all this land around here, including this house.'

Mrs Ennismore showed me around the great square principal reception rooms which had recently been re-decorated and furnished. They were decorated in fashionable 'London' colours – holly green, beef red and chocolate, and there were a number of expensive-looking velvet button-back armchairs and sofas, all recently refurbished.

She said: 'He lived here over a hundred years ago, but around here people still tell stories about Robert George Luxton – it's amazing: he was chiefly famous for drink, debauchery and gambling.'

We drank coffee in a vast stone-flagged kitchen overlooking a range of deserted stables and an empty Dutch barn. 'I don't think we are going to go on living here,' she said bleakly. 'We don't really belong. It takes years to get to know Devonians.'

I drove over to Okehampton late that morning to visit the estate agents who were handling the sale of West Chapple.

Okehampton is a stolid moorside town, reminiscent of

hardy communities in the north of England; most of its commercial buildings are constructed of pale grey stone and there is a bracing atmosphere of Nonconformity. The people appear austerely dressed and grimly polite: solid, prosperous chapels stand at every corner alongside the high-street banks.

A man talked guardedly to me in the offices of Dobbs, Stagg and Knowlman. He said that the Luxtons' property had been on the market for about six months before their death. It was still on the market, and the beneficiaries could not be named until the order of the deaths had been established to everyone's satisfaction.

I asked him who the beneficiaries might be, but over and over again he wanted my assurance that I was not a journalist. 'We've had enough of journalists. We're shutting the doors on them now,' he said emphatically. 'I didn't like the way they patted us on the head as if we were rustic and quaint. Some of them were extremely snide, too.' At length he said: 'There's no family left. They were the last of the line.'

He confessed that the Luxtons had agonized over the sale of the property. 'Robert the eldest was failing in health, and Frances didn't have an ounce of flesh on her. They just couldn't cope. On the other hand Alan was reluctant to sell: he was a recluse, and there was some story or other there. It led to fights between them all. Then Robert and Frances kept phoning us and the solicitors, and they kept changing their minds.'

When I asked if I could enter the house he said that the keys were with the Luxtons' solicitors at the offices of J. J. Newcombe.

At Newcombe's I met with a barrage of silence. 'Any inquiries should be made in writing,' a receptionist told me frostily.

*

When I returned to Winkleigh after lunch the rain had stopped. I went along to Inch's cider factory a little way out of the village on the road towards West Chapple Farm. A sharp stench of rotting apples filled the air. Fred Lyne, the Luxtons' former farm labourer, was dressed in outsize black oilskins and was shovelling apples on to a rattling conveyor belt. He stopped work and faced me with startled blue eyes. He was short and lean, and a broken nose gave him the appearance of a bantam-weight boxer. He had a three-day growth of rimey beard and his cheeks were a rosy mass of broken capillaries. He thought I had come from the Social Security office and seemed disappointed when I asked him about the Luxtons.

'I can't talk here I'm afraid. Come and see me at home and I'll tell you what I can.' His manner was obliging and he had a quiet pleasant voice. We arranged to meet later that evening.

As I continued along the lane towards West Chapple Farm the sun shone warmly and the steep meadows were fresh and green after the rain. The entrance to the farm was situated off an unclassified road four miles from Inch's factory. A long deep lane, so overshadowed that it was like a continuous bower, led to a five-barred gate, and beyond this across a silent meadow was an ancient stone cottage, green to the very door. The place seemed deserted, and many seeking West Chapple Farm itself must have turned back, convinced that there could be no human habitation beyond the primitive gate at the side of the building. I left my car by the cottage and went on through this second gate to another track that descended rapidly into a combe. To the left were steep woods with beech and oak trees; on the right was a fast-running stream softly murmuring through mirror-smooth green meadows that ended in a wooded rise with a line of lofty chestnut trees. The hidden access, the sense of seclusion, had a strange effect on me, as of slipping back into the past, into early childhood. The combe was full of birdsong and there were paired sea-mews wailing wildly in the distance. The trees in the thick copses were astir, sometimes yielding, sometimes parting in the wind.

At length the track rose to a bluff where there was a second gate leading into a cobbled yard, with a low-lying thatched house to the right and huge granite barns to the left. There was an impression of stillness, of great age; the air was sweet and clean, the high moors rose blue and purple in the west. The sunshine lay warm and cheerful on the primitive dry-stone yard wall.

The windows of the house were small with lace half-curtains. There were two doorways with storm porches. One of them had an ornate fretwork gate. Bright green moss was speckled with sun on the glistening cobbles, and grass grew up through the reed-roofed dovecote at the end of the yard.

As I cupped my hands to look through the first set of windows a rough voice startled me from the side of the house. 'What are you doing?'

A thickset man had materialized suddenly in the yard. He had a shining, almost oriental face, massive shoulders, and hands and wrists fit to wrestle with an ox. He was dressed in working clothes and a greasy cap sat squarely on his massive battering-ram of a head. He approached me with a steady, authoritative step until we stood face to face.

When I told him that I was interested in the property, possibly as a buyer, he was immediately relieved and all smiles. 'You can't be too careful around here,' he said.

We fell to talking, and this much seemed clear through his thick accent, which sounded East European overlaid with broad Devon: his name was Danovitz, and he was a Ukrainian refugee who had come to Britain after the war. He had worked at a refugee centre in Huddersfield and finally ended up in Winkleigh in 1956, working for the Luxtons. He hinted that it had suited him well to live in virtual hiding. Like Fred Lyne, he had been given a week's notice before their deaths, and as he lived in the tied cottage at the entrance to the farm he was anxious that a new owner should be found and that he should be re-employed.

Why was it, I asked him, that he had not been mentioned in any of the newspaper accounts?

'Oh, I stayed well out of sight,' he said. 'Well out of sight.'

He could not show me inside the house as the place was locked up and the solicitors had the keys. 'They've taken everything away. All the papers and money. Thousands of pounds, all over the place. They've put it all away safely.'

He proceeded to give me an impromptu tour of the out-buildings. Beyond the house was a set of low barns and sheds. 'Look at this,' he said, proudly leading the way. We stood in front of a fantastic contraption, twelve feet high and built of ancient wood and leather. 'That's an old cider-press still in working order. And through there after you've turned out the rubbish you could make a wonderful workshop.'

My eyes strayed with fascination and curiosity over great stacks of old paper, yellowing and dust-laden, and hundreds of mouldering boxes stacked to the very ceiling.

'What's this?' I asked, picking up one of the bundles.

'Put that down,' ordered Danovitz. 'Don't touch anything. You wouldn't be interested in any of that, it's just rubbish. They never threw anything out. They even saved the wall-paper they stripped off the walls.'

Coming out again into the yard, he said: 'They were mean, I tell you. I once walked through here with an apple my wife give me for lunch. Robbie say I steal it from his bloody orchard. I say them apples of yorn are cider apples: this apple be a sweet 'un. "Be it sweet, eh?" he said. "We'll soon see." He grab it, took a bite, and give it back without a word of sorry.'

We walked on past the orchard where the apples lay in profusion in the grass. Through another gate lay a track with damp clay banks, furred with mould. This led to a deep and solemn pool surrounded by immense beech trees. Beyond this stood an ancient and deserted house now used as a barn. 'This house belong to Alan,' said Danovitz. 'It's called Lute House. During the war evacuees live 'ere – a man with twelve children. You could do it up nice. Very solid still, very good property.'

On the way back we entered a wicket gate at the side of the main farmhouse and came out on to a sloping garden with overgrown lawns and flowerbeds running down to a low hedge. To the left by the orchard fence was a neglected vegetable patch. Danovitz pointed to a spot between the fence and a row of blackened stakes. 'That's where they found them,' he said.

This side of the house was clearly the main façade: it had open and delightful views across the combe to the moors beyond. The downstairs windows were deep and Georgian with red curtains. Above there was a trellis with dying roses – they had not been pruned for several years. There was a garden seat against the wall of the house. I noticed that a window was slightly ajar on the first floor and I longed to go in.

As we stood looking up at the house I asked where the various members of the family slept.

Danovitz rubbed his nose and indicated firmly that he was ignorant of those sort of arrangements.

He turned and looked out towards the fields as if signalling a change of subject.

When I pressed him further he made it clear that it was none of his business to know that sort of thing, and none of my business to ask.

He now led the way through a wicket gate in the garden to

a low shed. He opened the door and waited in silence for my reaction. As I grew accustomed to the darkness within I suddenly recoiled with vertigo. A deep pit had been dug in the ground to insert the huge cast-iron water-wheel mentioned by the reporters in the newspapers. One could easily have walked into the shed and dropped thirty or forty feet to the underground culvert below. The wheel, which Danovitz assured me had been used until quite recently, drove a Victorian thresher and crusher in the barns.

Back in the yard he pointed to an incline paved with flagstones. 'That's where they found Alan,' he said. 'You can still see blood, it don' go away.'

We examined the hideous dark stain that seemed to have impregnated the stone permanently.

That evening after a glass of beer and a light supper at the King's Arms I set off in the dark to find Fred Lyne's house. The street lighting was primitive and there was a smell of autumn bonfires in the air. The Lynes lived in a terrace of cottages down a steep passageway. One had to negotiate a worn flight of stone steps in the pitch darkness to reach the front door, which opened straight into the living room.

There were a few pieces of wooden furniture painted black – an old settle and table. A grandfather clocked ticked noisily in a dim corner. The Lynes huddled over a meagre coal fire. Fred's wife was a grey little lady who hardly looked at me once. She rocked gently in her great old horsehair armchair and stared into the fire.

I found Fred a gentle, intelligent man, torn between sorrow over the Luxtons' deaths and anger at the way in which he'd been dismissed without compensation after a lifetime's work. There was something very ripe about him, compassionate and resigned.

'I got two weeks' holiday a year. Every day off was marked down, just as their father had done, and I suppose his father before him. I was a bell-ringer over at Broadwood Kelly. On particular days I'd ring bells for saints' days, or weddings or a funeral. The deceased might have been one of their own relatives, but they'd dock the day off my holidays.

'Bell-ringing is part of the life of the countryside, it's not a hobby like golf or football. If you could hear the bells here from Broadwood Kelly, they'd say it was a sign of rain.

'In her father's day there would be four men working on that farm. We did it with just two of us, me and Danovitz, with no change in the methods right up to the end. They were living as they lived a hundred years ago. There was no pleasure. It was all work. They would be out with lanterns working with the beasts until bedtime. They didn't want to give up. The land was very good, but needed so much work the way they did it. They were tired, they couldn't go on. She saw the sense of giving up and getting out. But it would never do. They had old-fashioned sheep and cattle: old Ruby Reds and Long-wools – like you used to see before the war. They sold a lot to Sam Lendon up at the abattoir, we used to drive the cattle up there on foot. They used to sell to the North Devon Meat Company as well. A lorry would come and take the beasts away. You see the Luxtons never had a vehicle for transport-ing animals. In the old days they'd drive the cattle as far as Hatherleigh or Okehampton. In the end they sold off the stock, then they changed their minds and wanted it all back.

'Sometimes I got to work wet through with the rain. I never got a cup of tea even in the coldest day in winter. Every day I had to eat my dinner out in the shed. They never gave me a shilling extra or a bite to eat. Mind you, towards the end I wouldn't have fancied what the boys ate anyway. Towards the end I saw them eat lettuce sandwiches and rock cakes that weren't fit for the cattle.

'They weren't always so bad. Alan had gone courting but the engagement was broken off. Later he had some kind of breakdown and became a bit mental. He used to keep to his room for days on end. Then he would come out and shout and yell at us.

'During the last few months Danovitz and I did most of the work. They stayed inside; sick they were, like sick animals who've crawled away to die. A sale was arranged and the buyer, a farmer from down in Kent, had agreed on a price. All the stock was sent away except for two cows with calves to give milk for the house. They were to sign the contract with the buyer and move out by Michaelmas. But the sale was never completed. They belonged in the past; like some old tree they just couldn't survive being uprooted.'

After leaving the Lynes I decided on impulse that I would return to West Chapple Farm to see inside the house. From my Ordnance Survey map it appeared that the bridle path would take me down past the abandoned Lute House and into West Chapple farmyard from the opposite direction to the official entrance. I drove back past Inch's cider factory and parked my car by a field gate at the entrance to the bridle path. Armed with a flashlight I set off for West Chapple. It was a dark moonless night. I very soon had reason to regret this method of approach. After years of neglect the path was overgrown with brambles and nettles; in the recent rains it had become waterlogged. After slipping up to my shins in mire and tearing my hands in blackberry bushes I decided to walk across the fields. This was hardly a better decision. The Luxtons' neighbours, at least, were initiated into the use of barbed wire and I ripped a good pair of trousers in three places plunging through reinforced hedges; to add to my discomfort a sense of guilt transformed every oddly shaped tree or curious cow into a fearful apparition. For an hour or more I was com-

pletely lost and floundering in a boggy wood. The only reason
I persevered at all was that I did not know my way back. But
at length I came out past Lute House and the black pond and
entered the farmyard. I stood for a long while in the dark until
I was satisfied that nobody was about. I had suspected that the
police or even the solicitors might well have posted a night-
watchman, but he would surely move around or sit inside a
lighted room.

I tried the two yard doors and finding them locked went
through a wicket gate and round the side of the house to try
the garden doors. All were solidly locked, but to my delight I
found that a window into the dairy had already been forced,
and it gave way with a gentle push. I stood listening at the
window for several minutes, then climbed inside.

Beyond the dairy I switched on the flashlight and found
myself in an ancient kitchen with blackened oak settles and a
scrubbed deal table. The plaster walls, once white, were aged
to a dark ivory. The floor was paved with slate tiles and in the
corner was a granite brine bath. There were still groceries on
the shelves – a packet of salt, porridge oats, soap powder.

There were two downstairs reception rooms, both gloomy
and smelling of damp. The wallpaper looked as if it had been
up since before the First War. Much of the furniture was stout
and simple, nineteenth-century stuff in oak and elm. There
was a good grandfather clock by A. Allgood of Ledbury – the
pendulum lay frozen with dust. There was a pleasant little
Victorian loo table and a beautifully made travelling chest.
There was a chesterfield, some old wicker chairs, and several
armchairs covered in faded chintz. There was not a stitch of the
twentieth century in the house; these were the household goods
of a prosperous early-nineteenth-century farmer, complete with
dingy oleographs of rural and Biblical scenes, heavy damask
curtains, hideous antimacassars and a profusion of brasses,
tulip-shaped coloured glass vases and moralistic samplers:

Pleasures are like poppies spread
You seize the flower its bloom is shed
Or like the snowfall in the river
One moment there then gone forever.

And again more sombre yet:

By much slothfulness
the building decayeth
And through idleness of hands
the house droppeth through

There was a bookcase with a selection of old family Bibles gathering dust and some theological and devotional works, including a well-thumbed copy of Paley's *Evidences* and *The Imitation of Christ* by Thomas à Kempis.

Upstairs I found three bedrooms in use. The master bedroom with a massive eighteenth-century double bed evidently belonged to one of the brothers. The bed looked as if it hadn't been made for ten years and there were soiled clothes in heaps all over the place. A cast-iron safe stood open and empty.

The two other rooms had single beds. The one looking out over the garden had obviously been used by Frances. Dresses that had been fashionable forty years ago were hung over a chair. There was a faded photograph in a silver frame of a man and woman I took to be her parents. There was a washstand with a bowl and cracked pitcher, a commode with a cane back.

The third bedroom was filthy, with heaps of rags and sacking and piles of rotting newspaper and binder twine. I sensed an atmosphere of bitterness and despair; there was an overpowering, evil stench. Standing in that frightful room I felt a sudden urge to get out of the house. I went downstairs immediately and climbed out through the window into the garden. I decided to walk back to my car by the normal exit from the farm. It was a half-mile walk down the track to the final gate by Danovitz's cottage, and the road. The wind rushed noisily in the turbulent trees above me and I felt a childish sense of fear.

I got back to Headlands Manor at midnight, but the brothers were still up and eager to hear about my progress. They were fascinated, and clearly a little horrified, to learn that I had entered the house, and questioned me very closely about the sleeping arrangements. Derek said that there was a strong rumour about Winkleigh that Frances and Robbie had been lovers.

We sat up till the early hours of the morning theorizing about the Luxtons. Then, just before we went to bed, Christopher, who ran the farm at Headlands, spoke up. Up till now he had sat in silence listening intently and smoking one cigarette after another. He said: 'It's the sort of thing that happens when you worry too much about the past, or too much about the future. Or, worst of all, about what people think and say. What's the point in being frantic about things: you'll be dead soon enough and it's all over, too late. You can spend every day of your life labouring from dawn till dusk on a farm. You can get into debt and worry yourself sick. But at the end of the day you're no better off than if you'd just let it all take care of itself. The animals know where they want to eat, just leave them to it and let them wander. They know how to survive.'

At half past two Derek said: 'How about a hand of bridge before we turn in.' He was rather disappointed when I declined.

In the morning I wrote letters in every direction, including notices to newspapers at home and abroad asking for information about the Luxtons. I wrote to Newcombes the solicitors and to Mr Brian Luxton in Barry. I was still writing at eleven o'clock when the brothers appeared sleepy-eyed from their beds and cooked a gargantuan breakfast of home-cured bacon, eggs, tomatoes, freshly picked mushrooms and fried bread.

At midday Christopher wandered off to tinker about in the farmyard and Derek announced: 'As we have a guest with a car I think I'll go to work today.'

Driving through the narrow lanes to the Barnstaple road, Derek explained that he had a rather vague job. 'You see, Chris looks after the farm, so I thought I'd better have a job. But I rarely get to it because the cars never work. I act as financial adviser to a contractor, although I must say I spend most of my time baby-sitting and cleaning the house.'

About three miles beyond North Tawton we turned off the road and into a driveway so overgrown that Derek had to get out of the car and beat back the branches and brambles.

At length we came out into a clearing before a decaying seventeenth-century house. There were children and dogs on the lawn and a beautiful young woman came over to greet us.

'Catastrophe!' she called out, laughing.

She led us round the side of the house where several men stood scratching their heads and staring into a great hole in the ground. One of them, a stocky little man with white hair, was Derek's employer. He explained that the nuclear fall-out shelter had completely filled up with rain-water. What was more, he had just discovered that the shelter was threatening the foundations of the house, which was even now in danger of collapsing into the hole.

'Oh God,' said Derek. 'If I'd known this I would have gone to play tennis.'

I made my excuses and left for Exeter.

After posting my letters I bought a supply of tapes to record interviews. Then I went to the Exeter Records Library and asked for information on Winkleigh. There was a very slight

file and I read it in less than an hour. There were notes about
two Norman castle-sites in the village, one giving its name to
Castle Street, the other to Croft Mount. It appeared that they
had been fortified manor houses rather than proper castles. A
note in the file claimed that Winkleigh's castles had been
associated 'with many a late remembrance of dragons and
fairies'. Much of the information in the file was irrelevant to
my purpose, although it supported the contention that the
Luxtons had been a prominent family in the district for many
centuries. I read, for example, that they had inhabited the
nearby manor of Holcombe in the sixteenth century and that
in various church affairs at Winkleigh and Brushford Barton
they had been generous benefactors.

Among a sheaf of newspaper clippings was an intriguing
story of local politics. In 1936 the village had been divided
over whether a community hall should be built on the site of
Croft Mount, the Norman castle-site mentioned above. For
two years the village elders wrangled over the matter and the
entire population took sides. The Luxtons' father had put his
signature to a Parish Council resolution that opposed the
building of the hall. The site in question was a knoll in the
centre of the village with tall elms housing a rookery. Local
historians claimed that there were earthworks beneath dating
from the Bronze Age, 3,000 years ago, and that the Saxons, as
well as the Normans after them, had fortified the place with
wooden pallisades. As an indication of the arguments that
flew to and fro there was a cutting of this letter from a
Mr M. B. Norman in the *Western Morning News* of 26 July
1938:

Tradition has it that there is a secret passageway connecting the
two mounds, also that a carriage drawn by headless horses passes
under the village. There is an old warning that those who tamper
with the house of the rook are courting disaster. We would rather see

our Croft Castle crowned with trees and inhabited by friendly
rooks than crowned with any superfluous village hall.

The hall-builders, inevitably, won the day.

I took down the standard reference books – Welford's
County Families, White's, Kelly's and Billings's directories for
the second half of the nineteenth century. They disclosed that
in 1567 a Bernard Luxton purchased Holcombe Manor from
Sir Amyas Pawlet, and that it was still in the possession of the
Luxtons in the mid nineteenth century. White's Directory
(1850) recorded that Brushford Barton was a farm of 2,000
acres and had been owned by the Luxton family 'since the reign
of Elizabeth, previous to which the manor and tithes belonged
to Hartland Abbey'. In Kelly's (1893) I found that in the area
of Winkleigh the Luxtons had owned Hill Farm, Ridestone
Farm, West Chapple and Higher Reve; there were also three
farms in the vicinity taking their names from the Luxtons:
Luxton Barton, East Luxton and West Luxton. The text books
were disappointing on the origin of the Luxton name: the
supposition was that it derived from a Winkleigh man called
Lugg who was a figure of some importance in the thirteenth
century.

The censuses for 1841, 1851 and 1861 gave full details of
large Luxton families resident in the above farms, and by 1871
the West Chapple census return had recorded the arrival of
Frances's father, Robert John, who was then just one year old.
West Chapple was described as a 230-acre farm; the head of
household was Lawrence Luxton, who employed two men and
two boys. He was married to Mary and his three children were
Fanny, Mary Louisa and Robert John. There were visitors
in the house, William Kelland and Louisa Kelland, both
described as 'scholars'. There was a John Knight, aged
eighteen, described as a servant.

*

Several people had told me that I should go to see Sam Lendon. After my stint in the library I set off to find him back in Winkleigh. Sam, who was in his eighties, was a farmer and wholesale butcher and knew everybody in Winkleigh. He now lived in retirement up near the old airfield on the Torrington road. His place was not easy to find. The entrance to Ashlea Bungalow was secreted off a fast straight road. I came eventually to a smart new bungalow surrounded by post-and-rail fencing. As I entered the driveway a lean, wizened old man in bifocals came out of the front door in his stockinged feet. It was Sam.

He peered at me intently and suspiciously for some time before inviting me inside. He very much wanted to talk about the Luxtons. In the hallway there were red wall-to-wall carpets and the walls were painted in bright colours. He took me into the sitting room where there were three youths lounging in front of a huge colour television set. They stood up at once and departed without a word. Sam turned off the set and we sat opposite each other, in comfortable modern armchairs. Looking out of the window across the meadows he launched at once into a monologue.

'I can't understand it. I can't understand it at all. I'll never understand why they did it. They were strong people, full of character and good Christians. It wasn't like them to do such a thing unless it was Alan who was entirely to blame. He was different. He was a bit mental. I think he was spoilt, especially by Frances. As he was the youngest she treated him as a bit of a lollipop. I knew them all their lives, you know, and I knew their father too. I'm so old, I once saw Robert George Luxton the Squire over at Brushford.

'I had an abattoir in Winkleigh and I was a farmer, too. After the war I moved the business up here on to the airfield. But all my life I bought meat from the local farmers. I've bought meat from the Luxtons for nearly seventy years. They would drive their sheep or pigs along the lanes to me, always good animals they kept. They were good farmers, but old-fashioned. They were the last around here to farm with horses. Kept four horses, a brood mare for the trap and three for working. I never knew them socially; they weren't the type to mix and to tell you the truth I didn't mix much myself. I used to be a bit of a drinking man before the war, but the war stopped all that. I lost all my friends because of the war. When the Americans and the Canadians came to the airfield they used to crowd out the pubs in Winkleigh. They'd spill right out into the market place. You'd get a thousand of them in Winkleigh all trying to get a drink at once. Well, all the old locals stopped going to the pub; I lost all my friends in that way.

'The Luxtons were never drinking people but I had a great admiration for them. They were very tight, but they weren't as tight as me, I can tell you. They were absolutely straight, scrupulously honest, paid absolutely on the nail. But they weren't mean, no, they were just careful. But you have to be in farming.

'The great tragedy of that family was that none of them married. Had they married none of this would have happened. But whether they felt that nobody was good enough for them, or what – they never got round to it. I knew Alan had a go – got engaged – but it never worked out.

'The Lord bless us and have mercy on us! To think of them all dead; so many of my old friends are dead now. It's funny talking about the war; I've just remembered something I haven't thought about in years and years. On the day the war ended the celebrations resulted in near-calamity on my farm. I was farming up here, and I had a lovely herd of fifty dairy cattle. I had three land girls, as they called them at that time: big strong girls who'd do anything. Well, they weren't sup-posed to do this, because they were on a kind of national service, but when it was announced that the war was over they disappeared to Winkleigh for a party, then they went off home to Brighton and London and wherever they came from. I had a labourer who did the same, too. Well I was left with fifty cows to milk and I'd never milked a cow before in my entire life. So I started milking them at quarter to four in the morning and I was still milking at three o'clock in the afternoon, and I just kept going like that right round the clock until I managed to get someone to help me out.

'What I'll never understand as long as I live is how the Luxtons lost all their money. The stories you used to hear about that family back at the beginning of the century – the farms they had, and the houses. But it all went. I remember myself riding to hounds with old "Gus" Luxton when I was a little boy. They called him Squire Luxton too, like his father. As a boy I've ridden along behind old "Gus" all the way from Eggesford to Okehampton to a meet. God bless and save us, how the years vanish!'

Sam Lendon told me that I should talk with Mrs Tadbold. She had been friendly with the Luxtons for at least thirty years, using their sheep dip and the crusher in the barn. She now lived in retirement on the Hatherleigh road five miles out of Winkleigh.

Her bungalow was set back off the road beyond a bleak, windswept garden. The woodwork was painted a melancholy kingfisher blue. I peered through the front window into a room furnished with only a single camp bed. After I rang the doorbell Mrs Tadbold came to this window and stood with it a little ajar. She was not inclined to let me in. She was a little dumpling of a woman with wispy hair, and of great age. Her face was covered in a thousand fine wrinkles, vermilion at the cheeks, and her coal-black eyes were buried deep above fleshy high cheek-bones.

At length, mention of Sam Lendon convinced her that I had some stake among the locals and she told me to go round to the kitchen door.

A weed-ridden path led to a cinder patch at the back of the house. There were clear views out over the meadows and no visible neighbouring habitation in the landscape. A pile of chopped wood lay by the step and inside the door were several pairs of muddy Wellington boots. I sat at Mrs Tadbold's kitchen table and she made me a cup of tea while she talked. Her cat leapt up and down at a fly buzzing against the window over the sink.

'I was walking along the lane and a car came racing along at high speed. It screeched to a stop and a man opened the window. I suppose he was a reporter or something. He said: "Do you know where the farm is where the people were shot?" I said: "Which people?" And he said: "Two brothers and a sister." Well I knew straight away who he meant and I collapsed there and then; I just passed right out and fell into the hedge.

'I'll never understand why they did it. They were such good Christians. They had a terrible reputation for meanness, but they were more generous than anyone could possibly have imagined. My son is deaf and always had difficulties. Every year at Christmas Robbie used to come up here on the white pony – that's how he and Frances used to get around. He'd come on Christmas Eve or on Boxing Day and give me ten shillings for my boy. He used to do the same for children of some others around here. Now he'd stand outside and talk and talk and nod, smiling at my boy, but he wouldn't come in. It was the same every year. First of all I'd say come on in for some dinner; it was usually midday, you see. But he'd nod towards West Chapple and say: "Oh no, I've got my dinner keeping back home." And he'd stand talking and smiling for an hour more. We used to laugh about that. You wouldn't see him

again like that until the next Christmas came round. I think
he really loved children and missed them in his life.

'They worked too hard for socializing, and it was all old gear
they had. They even made their own paint – now that's
something that went out a hundred years ago. They concocted
it with a special clay, and any lime left over from what they
used in the fields went on the walls of the house or the barns.
Nothing wasted. People say they were hard on their workers,
but they were careful and fair. One of my own workers wanted
to work on during his holidays and get paid double for the
week. He needed some extra money. I told Robbie about it
and he said I should refuse to do it. He said it would throw
everything out of balance. The man wouldn't have a proper
rest, for a start, and where was the extra money to come from?
He said the next thing was they'd start asking for longer
holidays and shorter working days and it would be double
every five minutes. Robbie couldn't stand progress; he never
believed in progressing onwards in any sense.

'I know that Alan had some illness in the fifties. I think he
might have had an ulcer or something; he was quite different
from the other two. Robbie and Frances were like hand in
glove. Robbie explained to me that Frances was all for moving
to Crediton and making a home for the boys, but Alan was all
for staying. Alan suggested that they should go off to Crediton
together and leave him behind as their tenant. Just imagine
Alan all alone on that farm. Most days he never got up until
five o'clock in the afternoon. He asked Fred Lyne if he'd stay
on and work for him, but Lyne said "No!"'

Back in Winkleigh, through the Lynes, I came to meet
Rosemary Dark, a large old lady in a floral housecoat who
lived in a thatched cottage down a steep cobbled lane running
away from the village square. The living room of the cottage
was spotlessly clean and polished, and as she spoke to me she

constantly fiddled with a duster, shaking it out and re-folding it neatly and nervously polishing the already mirror-like surface of the sideboard. She was a war widow and photographs of her husband in naval uniform lined the sideboard.

'Have you talked to Lionel Butler, at the post office? I shouldn't talk with him if I were you, or take any notice. He's only lived here about twelve years and he's already talking to the newspapers as if he's an expert. Well the fact is that the Luxtons reaped their reward, her in particular. Nobody around here will tell you the full story, but there are plenty of us know what we know and we're keeping it to ourselves. There are people here have known them all their lives, and their father and grandfather. I knew her mother Wilmot, who was a Short. But of course the Luxtons thought themselves a cut above the Shorts. They had no truck with the village, and poor old Wilmot wasn't allowed to have her own family up to Chapple. Frances was too proud of course to come to church here at Winkleigh. It was always over at Brushford she went so that she could act the lady of the manor, no doubt. Now you know why she was buried over there instead of with her own mother and father and brothers in Winkleigh. Can you beat that? Snobbery beyond the grave! And if there was no service there and she had to come up here she'd always dash out the side so that she wouldn't have to speak to the likes of us. Makes me laugh these people: always go to church they do, no matter how they behave. Well, we have our own ideas about her and Robbie. It ran in the family that did. And it's my thinking that's how the family came to grief. You've never known so much intermarrying, one after the other marrying cousins and aunts and nephews and what have you, and carrying on with each other.'

As she spoke, Mrs Dark became flushed with emotion. She rocked slightly, to and fro, with the vehemence of her monologue.

She went on to hint that intermarriage over the generations had affected Alan.

'Now you see. That's why Alan was a bit touched. The genes
need fresh blood to be healthy and sane. Well, they must have
suffered terrible guilt living as they did. A family that inter-
marries like that and carries on gets a curse on it. Just look at
that family: wiped off the face of the earth they were and look
at their end – could you think of a more terrible retribution?

'I don't care who killed who, or did what to who, but it
wasn't a good death, was it? It was a curse working its way out.
In the olden days the vicar would not have allowed a proper
church burial. Now what would Lionel Butler know of all
these things? You've got to know a family and country ways
over years and years. There's so much I could tell you, but it's
no business of mine. It may sound wicked to say it, but it's a
mercy they're dead and buried. That's how I see it. I mean
there was the other business that no decent Christian should
have dealings with: visits to the churchyard at night, muttering and talking to the graves. What was all that about? You
wouldn't believe it would happen in this day and age in the
world of television and aeroplanes and going to the moon.
Well you wouldn't say it was healthy and normal, would you?
But ever since she was a girl she couldn't be like the rest.
Always had to be different.'

On leaving Mrs Dark I took a short cut through Winkleigh
churchyard to the village square and ran into the vicar. He
was a soft-spoken Welshman called John Williams, but he had
been brought up in North Devon and had spent the last three
years as parish priest of Winkleigh. I was intrigued that
nobody seemed to have helped them in their depressed state
during the weeks before their death. 'They were quiet people,'
said John Williams. 'She and Robbie came regularly to
Brushford, which is more or less a defunct congregation. I must

say I didn't realize that Robbie was in such a state. Alan, of course, was completely mad – there was some love affair in the poor fellow's life which was thwarted. I'm really sorry for poor Frances – she had to manage two unhinged brothers without any help from outside. All three of them kept themselves to themselves and I don't know of anybody who visited them on a regular basis. They lived very simply and they didn't appear to spend any money on themselves.'

He apologized for not being able to help further and went off down the shingle path humming sadly to himself.

On the outskirts of the village, on the road to North Tawton, there is a little close of council houses called Sunny View. Here I met Mrs Chambers, who had been at school with Frances in the village fifty years earlier. I found her standing at her door. Her husband, a farmworker, was in the kitchen and we went in to talk.

She said: 'Money, money, money lay at the root of it. They had a great-uncle who was a big landowner and wealthy. He was a drinker and a gambler; he broke his neck falling from a horse. Memories go back a long way on the land. The Luxtons were a big family in these parts; many of them lost their livelihoods and went abroad. The grandfather blamed it all on drinking, gambling and spending. He was desperate that nothing should be wasted. Every penny earned should be saved, nothing should leave the farm. The three children were brought up in this atmosphere. Marriage was discouraged because the wives might be spenders, money would leave the farm. As time went on Robbie became worse than his father; and Frances was even worse than him towards the end.

'Frances owned a cottage in Winkleigh. A year or two ago the tenants wanted to get rid of a dreadful old broken-down cooking range. Frances wouldn't agree until they said they'd bear the cost themselves. But she insisted that all the rusted bits of iron from the old range should be returned to West Chapple Farm: nothing should be wasted, you see!

'She could be very uppity and superior towards the end. A workman passed her in the lane and saluted her, but she just walked on past him as if he didn't exist. She was a lovely girl when she was young – a lovely complexion and auburn hair, but I think she felt there was something rather special about being a Luxton. I know it seems hard to believe, but when she was a girl she occasionally went walks with a young man. Her father was very jealous for her and used to follow her on horseback about fifty yards down the road.

'It was a model farm and they were wonderful farmers, but without proper agricultural machinery and without modern fertilizers they had to work harder than everyone else. Robbie was at it from six o'clock in the morning until twelve o'clock at night. Talk about self-sufficiency – even their furniture had been made at the farm, right there on the spot! Frances was the only one with outside interests, but they were rather peculiar. The only thing that interested her was graveyards and churches. Always rummaging around among the old gravestones. She'd sit there for hours among the graves. Just sit there and rock to and fro. They say she was working on their family history. In all these years I only ever went up there once – to get some cream. But she didn't invite me in. I was kept waiting at the door.'

The allegation of meanness was again contradicted by a conversation I had later that afternoon with a Mrs Dunn – one of those friendly women who are the backbone of the Women's Institute and the Parish Council. I met her in the Post Office and walked back to her house with her.

She said: 'Twice a year my husband and I would drive around the parish collecting cakes: in July for the church tea, and in the autumn for the Harvest Festival. Although we were never invited in, Frances always gave cheerfully and generously for church causes – both in money and other ways. This year was peculiar. We were kept waiting at the door a very long time. Robbie looked through the window and disappeared. Eventually Frances opened the door and gave us some money. She looked – oh, so very unhappy and thin. She asked us to do what we could for them. I took this to mean would we pray for them. I think Frances was a very good woman, quite holy in her way, but different and misunderstood. She used to leave church quietly and alone by a side door before the service was over to avoid meeting and talking with other people.'

In a cottage backing on to the churchyard I spoke with Mary Stannard. She was in her fifties and a contemporary of Alan's at the village school. She was making bread in the kitchen when I called on her, and at the kitchen table sat her parents who were in their eighties. They were both talkative and kept interrupting each other. The old man said that he had fought with the Devonshires in Palestine and at Gallipoli during the First War and had worked for 'Maister' Robert John Luxton as a boy before the First War. 'When I came 'ome he didn't wanna know me. But little Frances was good to me.' He chatted on, unaware of my tape recorder, while Grandma interrupted and contradicted. She had enormous spectacles with thick lenses. Sometimes she let out a great cackle and slapped her aproned lap. I think she was only remotely aware of what we were talking about. Eventually they both tottered off into the sitting room to watch horse racing on television, leaving Mary and myself alone.

'I knew Alan ever so well. He was a lovely boy, you know. He was so full of life, and *normal* – not like the other two. He was a lot younger than them, a different generation entirely. He used to belong to the Young Farmers, that's where I met him. He was always the life and soul, dancing and dashing about the place. Back home they treated him very badly. He was a part-owner of the farm, but they paid him farm labourer's wages. I don't know how he ever afforded anything, but he was always decently dressed in those days, smart and well-turned-out, proud of himself. Anyway, he fell in love with a girl from Hatherleigh called Myrtle. She's been happily married for years now and lives down in Exeter. But he was so much in love with her at the time, and he treated her like a princess. Anyway he proposed and she accepted and he gave her a beautiful ring. They were a lovely couple, really happy.

'Then the trouble started. He wanted to sell up his part of the farm and start up on his own – only natural, wasn't it? – but the other two said no. They prevented him. He was only earning about four pounds a week – this was after the war – he had nowhere to live and no job to go to. The rows were terrible between him and his sister and brother. They cheated him out of his due. Then one day he just gave up. He went down to Hatherleigh, asked for the ring back. He didn't say a word. He just knocked on her door, she gave the ring back and he turned on his heels. He gave no explanation, nothing. He never spoke to her again. She was so upset, she just couldn't understand. At first she thought it was something she'd done. He never explained what he'd done. It took her a long time to get over it. She just couldn't understand; she really loved him and I think he loved her.

'After that he stopped coming to the Young Farmers and never came to the pub. Sometimes his friends would go to call but he told them to bugger off. The next thing we heard he'd been taken ill and ended up in hospital with mental trouble. He was there a few weeks and when he came back you wouldn't have recognized him. I only saw him once or twice in Winkleigh. He let himself go completely – filthy dirty, never cut his hair, always needed a shave, and his clothes dreadful.

One day I saw him in the Post Office and waited for him to come out.

'I said, "How are you getting on then Alan?" And do you know what he said to me? He said "F— off!" I said, "No necessity for that, Alan." But he just walked off. I heard terrible stories of rows and everything. I heard Robbie and Frances used to lock him up. Well, look how it all ended. Everybody around here thinks that he murdered his brother and sister and then committed suicide. What a terrible thing to have done – I mean, your own brother and sister! But I think they ruined his life. And just think what that property must be worth? They must be worth a hundred thousand pounds each, and to think he couldn't afford to get married to the girl he loved. But in recent years Frances was gallivanting all over the world and spending money. That family have always been deep down mean. My old dad was starving for work when he came back from the trenches. He'd worked his fingers to the bone for their father before the First War, but he wouldn't take him back – there was no work. But at least my old dad managed to marry the woman he loved.'

Walking through the churchyard again I met Mrs Williams, the vicar's wife. We spoke for a little while standing by the brothers' grave. 'The Luxtons have no gravestones yet. Who is to pay for them? They had some cousins in Reading and I believe some money was left to them. The previous vicar but one would be very useful to talk to, I'm sure. He was a bachelor and used to play the violin.

'Frances was out of this world in her long navy blue coat and close-fitting hat. She used to sit in a side aisle when she came to church at Winkleigh, quite apart from the rest of the congregation. In my job as a pastor's wife I have to learn to get on with most folk, but she was quite impossible. And I never spoke a word to Robert.'

Was there nobody in the neighbourhood, I asked Mrs Williams, who might have ranked as a true friend of Frances or her brothers?

She thought for a while, then said: 'I can't really think of anybody, but I believe Mrs Molland knew Frances well when they were young.'

Mrs Molland lived in a bungalow on the road from Winkleigh to the disused airfield. It was situated behind a tall privet hedge. The garden was full of late pink and white roses and the front door was protected by a conservatory with dozens of pots of geraniums. Mrs Molland came to the door slowly. She had a round kindly face and silver-white hair. She said that she was only too happy to talk about the Luxtons.

We sat in a parlour looking out over open fields and drank tea.

'I was a farmer myself for many years. I had a dairy herd and I kept sheep. My husband and I worked together at it all our lives. I don't know why people keep on about the Luxtons being mean. Being a small farmer often gives that impression, I suppose. They were very honest, which is the important thing. If you ever went out there alone they'd invite you in, but if anyone came they didn't know, they would not. I used to go out collecting for the church with old Mrs Haig. Now because Mrs Haig was what Frances would have considered a "lady" she would always make us come through the front door and we'd be invited into their parlour. I don't think that front door would be opened again until we came around next year. If I came on my own, though, it was the side door and we'd talk in the kitchen.

'I knew them from when they were children; we were at the village school together. Now here's a curious thing. We both used to come too far to have our lunch at home, so we used to bring our lunch to school with us. I used to take my sandwiches and bottle of milk to eat at Mrs Blacksmith's. Frances would take her lunch to the Lanes at Linden House. Now I'll tell you an extraordinary thing. The Lanes were brother and sister and very close. Then one day they quarrelled – about some money matters, I should think. They said around here, "Oh well, Mr Lane won't be able to live without her." Anyway one night he went down to the Knapmans' with a gun and just shot her dead. Then he tried to shoot himself but made a mess of it. Wasn't that extraordinary? Mr Lane murdered his sister and tried to kill himself. And Robbie and Alan and his sister have been shot. Yet Robbie and Frances were very close, just like the Lanes. They were inseparable – like hen and chicken – where she'd go he'd go too.

'Not long before the tragedy Robbie came in to see me and he was very poorly. He kept saying: "I've come to see you." "Well," I said, "do come in, Robbie." And he looked uncared for, thin and neglected – which as a rule he generally wouldn't. He said, "I'm not too good." So I said, "What's the matter?" And he said, "I've had a sale and I regret it. Oh, I do regret it." I said, "Well never mind, 'tis a bit of a wrench. I've been through it and you'll be all right." So I said, "Why ever don't you come in, Robbie?" He kept saying he wanted to see me, and he was walking up and down the conservatory ... it was getting dark. He kept picking bits off the plants, he didn't know what he was doing. I had a friend in and she wondered what on earth he was up to. So then he said: "What are you going to do with that bungalow?" I had a bungalow for sale, you see. So I said it was for sale. "How many bedrooms?" "Two." "Oh, not large enough." He didn't say anything sensible, and he didn't come in, and he didn't go home.

'"I wanted to give you something," he said. "I wanted to give you a donation for the church." At last he took it out and kept rubbing it as if it was dirty. And it was a pound note. He didn't go even then. I didn't realize he was as ill as he was – I wish I had.

'My cousin came in while Robbie was standing there in the conservatory. She thought he was down and out. She thought he was a tramp. When he went off at last it brought tears to my eyes. I never saw him again. I saw Frances in the church-yard, though. She looked terrible. She was standing in the rain, just standing among the graves in the long grass, looking so agitated and unhappy. I said, "How are you, Frances?" And she said, "I don't know." I feel ever so sorry for her, because she must have suffered. No one knows what she suffered. I don't think they would cheat anyone. They were just very careful of everything. They couldn't help it.'

The Woods had lived at Brook Farm, bordering on the Luxtons' land, for fifteen years. They had come from Hampshire and were therefore considered strangers in the district.

In addition to offering bed and breakfast in the farmhouse they made extra money by letting two cottages, and there was a caravan site in the paddock next to the farmyard. They appeared hag-ridden from hard work.

Mrs Woods said: 'They were neighbours, but we didn't have time to socialize. Everybody seems to think there's bags of money and leisure in farming: well, it's not a bed of roses. In all those years we spoke only four times. But they were fascinated by us and the way we did things on our farm. They would stand in their fields and watch us from a distance. But if you waved, or walked over to speak, they'd vanish. I had a long conversation not long before they died. Some of our sheep escaped on to their land and I went through and spoke with Robbie. I said I was sorry to hear that they were leaving the farm and he said, "It's all a mistake, we shouldn't be going." He was upset and couldn't speak. He just stood there as if overcome with wretchedness and misery.

'After a while he said, "I'll get my sister." After the usual pleasantries she said, "The farm should never have been sold. We should die on the place." She repeated that so many times. She said, "We're the last generation of Luxtons to be on the farm: we should die on the place." I asked whether it had all been signed and settled, and she said, "Nothing has been signed yet." I asked her, "Couldn't you back out?" But she said, "It's all too late; we've sold up, we've sold the stock. We should die on the place ... I don't know where we're going."

'I asked her about the summer and what she had thought of it, but she said she hadn't seen it as she'd been busy turning out drawers.'

Through Mrs Molland I learned of the existence of a distant relative of the Luxtons called Arthur Knapman; his mother had been their aunt. He now lived in Okehampton, where I went to visit him. He was a stout man with a huge stomach and he lay wheezing and writhing on an old chaise longue beneath the lace curtains of the garden window. He had an assortment of notes about the family history on the backs of old envelopes and had been compiling a family tree. He told me again the story of the Lanes – the Luxtons' cousins who had suffered a similar tragedy many years earlier.

'Old Lane shot his sister in our house. He blew her head off with a shotgun. Then he tried to shoot himself with a shoe-lace on the trigger, but he failed. He shot away the side of his face and lived. Verdict was unsound mind.

'The Luxton killings were all over a grudge. Young Alan fell in love with a beautiful Winkleigh girl called Myrtle. He gave her a ring and everything and they were going to get married. Up till then Alan had been a fine boy and such a keen farmer. Lively, intelligent, good-humoured. But trouble started over the engagement. The elder two quarrelled with him over the ownership of the land. He wanted his share so that he could get married, but the other two wouldn't sell. The rows were terrible. Then he broke off the engagement and never saw her again. But he never forgot or forgave, and it affected him – drove him mad. So now when the elder two wanted to sell up he gave them hell, gave them bloody hell.

'Before the romance broke up there'd been an engagement party. I went to it. Alan had friends before that. But afterwards he never came outside the door. He carried his resentment right up to the end and when they wanted him to sell he wouldn't.

'After that he grew to hate women with all his heart and soul. Robbie told me Alan used to keep a scrap-book of cartoons and articles and jokes against women. He was callous and cold-hearted where women were concerned.'

Through a friend of Mary Stannard I was put in touch with Irene Brown, who had been on holiday with Frances in the sixties. She was a widow and lived in Hatherleigh.

Hatherleigh is an ancient market town situated on a steep hill about eight miles from Winkleigh. I went there on market day. Many of the houses are thatched and made of cob. Gnarled farmers in khaki coats walked through the porticoed market hall as if oblivious of the stallholders selling everything from clotted cream to buttons. They were merely taking a short cut from the tea-rooms to the cattle market, where the serious business of the day was under way.

I walked up the hill and went into the parish church. I sat for a while in a pew at the back. The walls had recently been whitened and the whole effect was light and fresh and airy with golden October light flooding through the clear glass windows. The dark granite piers along the nave leant outwards with great age.

Irene Brown's cottage was a short walk from the church-yard, and as I approached I caught a glimpse of her swiftly withdrawing from the window. In the same dark window was a yellowing notice announcing the sale of cream teas. The offer seemed rather half-hearted. The door opened at once as I knocked, and there was Mrs Brown, skinny and freckly, with gingery hair. I had to stoop to get through the low door and immediately found myself in a scantily furnished tea-room. There was coconut matting on the floor and two plastic-topped tables and some hard upright chairs. The walls were painted apple green which only served to emphasize the chill of the room and its empty black grate. There was a faded print of Exeter Cathedral on the wall.

She smoked heavily as we talked, and she preferred not to be recorded on tape. 'She was a very special person, Frances. Yes, I knew her at school, but I knew her much better later on after my husband died. We made contact again through Inter Church Travel which organizes pilgrimage holidays with a special religious interest. It used to be down Pall Mall in London, but they use the parishes as a way of contacting people. After my husband died I never thought I'd be interested in anything again. I forced myself to get away and I went and booked holidays with Inter Church several times. Then in 1966 I suppose it was, I went to Israel and Frances was on the tour. We joined the ship in Italy and went to Malta and Israel and Greece. Frances was a wonderful help to me, I can't tell you. She was a very good woman; I think she was very close to God and she understood things. She made a great difference to my life. She loved nature. She would just sit for hours looking at a beautiful scene and she noticed everything to do with the land. She was a wonderful person to be with. I have a very beautiful memory of her. We were on the ship from Genoa. I got up very early the first morning and we were sailing down the coast of Italy and the sun had just risen and lit up the mountains along the coast. It was so beautiful and peaceful and the sea was glassy and calm. The men were

washing down the deck with hoses, and as I walked round the
ship I came upon Frances sitting on a sort of box thing. She
was reading her Bible and every so often looked out across the
sea to the mountains; she looked so content. When she saw me
she said: "I've just been reading the Psalms; it all comes alive
in the Mediterranean." After the tour she never invited me to
Winkleigh, but she came to see me once or twice. I used to go
on about my problems and she listened. You see, I found it
very difficult to get over my husband's death and I had no idea
that she had sorrows. She always seemed amused by her
brothers. She used to say it was good for them to get on without
her. She felt a great responsibility about her family past. I just
wish I'd been able to help her in some way. But it's no use
regretting, is it?'

I talked with her for about two hours. As I made my farewell
on her doorstep, I remarked that there were others in Winkleigh who took a 'quite different view of Frances'.

'I shouldn't take much notice of all they say about her up
in Winkleigh,' she said. 'I've heard them. A lot of them were
jealous of Frances. You know how it is in villages. You've got
to join in with the rest like a sheep, otherwise they have it in
for you. I couldn't wait to get away from Winkleigh, everybody knowing your business and poking their noses in. They
all think she was mean, but she gave far more than any of them
could possibly imagine. And another thing, I don't think
Frances would ever have taken her own life or harmed anybody else. I think she must have had a terrible death, poor
thing. I can't bear to think how terrible her last hours must
have been. But I'm sure she died very close to God.'

I had almost given up hope of hearing from the Brian
Luxton whose name I had seen in the parish visitors' book at
Brushford Barton, when I received the following letter from
him.

The tragic deaths of the Luxtons at West Chapple brought to an abrupt end more than 600 years' occupation of Winkleigh by members of the family. I never met Frances and her brothers Robert and Alan but I knew of them through my friendship with their second cousin William John Luxton, C.B.E. Mr Luxton and I have traced their branch of the family back to the marriage of George Luxton and Elizabeth Dark at Coldridge on 19 July 1760, their great-great-great-grandparents. This George Luxton (1733–92) was the youngest son of Robert Luxton squire of Brushford Barton who died in 1753 aged 63.

Luxton, which is a curious blend, is the name of two places in Devon, one in the parish of Upottery and the other in Winkleigh. The first was Luggestone in 1313, and the second was Luggeston in 1346. Both must mean 'farm/place of (a man called) Lugg' and there was a man called Nicholas Lug in Winkleigh Hundred in 1238. Research has confirmed that the family came from Winkleigh and spread from there throughout Devon, the rest of England and abroad. In the reign of Elizabeth I (1566) Bernard Luxton of Winkleigh, yeoman, purchased the manor of Abbotsham which included Brushford Barton from Sir Amyas Paulett who incidentally was the gaoler to Mary Queen of Scots when she was imprisoned in England. The Luxton family continued at Brushford until early this century.

Today from Robert and Jane Luxton, who were married in 1704, I have traced several hundred descendants living in various parts of Britain and also in New Zealand, Australia, Canada and USA. The use of a rare name like Luxton provides a valuable insight into distribution and disbursement of families caused by economic trends and personal ambitions.

Many years ago as I was studying documents in the Society of Genealogists Library in London, I noticed an elderly gentleman studying the same documents. It transpired that he was another Luxton keen on genealogy and knew of my existence because he was tracing the same leads. He had a letter that I had sent to a Bishop George Luxton in Huron, Canada. He put me in touch with an Eleanor Luxton in Canada who had written two books, *Luxton's*

Pacific Crossing and *Banff – Canada's First National Park*. From them I learned that her grandfather William Fisher Luxton emigrated from the West Country to Canada in 1855. There he became the first teacher in Winnipeg and founded a newspaper, *The Winnipeg Free Press*, in 1872. He was also a member of the Manitoba State Legislature. Looking back over my notes, I discovered that he was baptized at Skilgate, Somerset, in 1843 and was related to me. Eleanor's father, Norman Kenny Luxton (1876–1962), crossed the Pacific in a Wabash Indian canoe alone in 1901 and later befriended the Blackfeet Indians who made him Chief White Eagle.

A few days later I heard from J. J. Newcombe the solicitors:

Dear Sir,
                    Re: Luxton, Chapple Farm

Thank you for your letter. We have no instructions to reveal any information to you.

                                        Yours faithfully,

                                        Anthony Cloke (signed)

Through the Shorts I was given the address of the second cousin mentioned in Brian Luxton's letter, William Luxton, who lived in Guildford. I wrote several times, but received no answer. In the end I got his number through Directory Enquiries and telephoned him. He sounded distant but courteous, and he repeated over and over again that he doubted whether he could tell me anything useful. All the same, he invited me to lunch at his home, dictating elaborate instructions about trains, taxis and my time of arrival.

William Luxton lived in an enclave of impressive villas called Abbotts Wood, near Guildford. Each house was situated in its own grounds off a private, gated road among tall box hedges and pine trees. He was a thickset Devonian with a Gothic-shaped bald head and a determined jaw. He and his wife Meg greeted me courteously but cautiously, took me into the drawing room and gave me a glass of sherry. There had been too much sensational journalism surrounding the case, he said. It had been a sordid end to a splendid family line – 'Wounds should now be allowed to heal.' I gathered he meant his own, for there were no other Luxtons of even remote relationship to be hurt by the deaths.

He told me that he had recently retired as Chairman of the London Chamber of Commerce after a career in law and business. His father had left Devon at the turn of the century. 'He ran away and became a butcher's boy in Exeter. Times were hard for a small farmer's younger son and there were no prospects. Then he came up to London where he studied to be an engineer. I was brought up in North London although my spiritual home was always in Devon. The family history has been my hobby, and in particular the Luxtons of Winkleigh. Frances was trying to piece together a history of her own from church records and gravestones, but you need more than that. I've got all the wills of the Devon Luxtons as far back as I could into the seventeenth century.

'There's a vast amount of other stuff belonging to Frances that the Okehampton solicitors sent me. It's all rather private – interesting in its own way, I suppose, but of dubious relevance to a family history.'

'May I see it?' I asked.

'It's much too extensive to make any sense of it by a brief look. And I don't know whether in principle I ought to let you see it anyway. I'll think about it. What sort of book had you in mind?' He eyed me carefully as I gave my answer.

I said: 'Lots of books have been written about villages and country communities, but I thought it would be interesting to write about one farming family – showing how they lived and how change and progress put unbearable pressures on them.' He looked dubious still, but slightly happier than before.

Over lunch he told me about his own correspondence with

Frances. 'She was a great letter-writer and we corresponded throughout our lives. She would start a letter at Christmas and go on adding to it for four or five months – so that what you got was a sort of journal letter in April and May which had started out as a thank-you letter for a batch of old magazines I'd sent her in December. I have another series of long letters she sent my sisters in Reading – same sort of thing.'

After lunch we walked up and down the garden and he told me of his visits to West Chapple over the years. 'When I was a boy I used to put my bicycle on the train and go down to Exeter. I used to tour Devon for two or three weeks. In those days, this was before the war, I used to get a great spread, a real Devon cream tea. Their old father was all right for about twenty minutes – all smiles and welcoming, but then he'd cloud over and you had to watch out.

'I got into the habit of calling regularly over the years. They were always pleased to see me, but I knew about Alan and I knew that things were going to pieces in the last few years.'

I asked him when he had last seen them.

'It was just a few weeks before they died. We were on holiday down there. Meg my wife dropped me off near the farm – they were often more forthcoming when I went alone – and I walked down to the house. All three of them, Frances, Robert and Alan, were there, and I spent about an hour talking to them about the sale of the farm. They hadn't been eating and they were thin and depressed. We sat in the kitchen. Frances had been going through the family papers and there was a great mass of yellowing paperwork all over the place. She and Robert seemed guilty at what they had done, as if they had betrayed the family. Yet all their lives had been leading up to this. Alan seemed exultant in a strange way. That was the last time I ever saw Alan. When I left I told them that I was going to stay in the area and I would call back before I left for London.

'I believe from Robert's behaviour and from what Frances had told me that he had had a nervous breakdown, but because the farm was so secluded he had not received any medical treatment. At the last moment they had changed their minds about the sale, but Robert felt that although they were not legally bound to go through with the sale it was a matter of honour with him that he should do so. In the time-honoured way of country folk the deal was to have been sealed on Michaelmas Day.

'On the Sunday, just over a week before they died, I called at the farm again. I didn't see Alan that time, just Frances and Robert. I stayed at the house for about one and a half hours. I tried to advise them not to continue with the sale of the farm, as that seemed the best solution. They were obviously upset and deeply depressed about the forthcoming move but I wasn't able to get through to them at all. I advised them to stay at the farm because I thought it was the best thing to do and that they could let out the land on grazing agreements. Robert would only answer by saying that things had gone too far to withdraw. They really didn't seem to know what they were going to do. I helped him fill out an application for his Old Age Pension and then I left. I didn't see Alan that morning, although I am quite sure he was about. He had seemed the most stable of the three of them when I had seen him the week before.'

After lunch we went to an upstairs bedroom where there were several boxes of documents. 'The Luxton material is all here. The stuff I've collected over a lifetime and the material Newcombes the solicitors passed on to me.'

'I'd love to look through it all,' I said.

'I bet you would.'

When I left he said, I thought sincerely, that he would consider helping me. But I doubted whether we had the same kind of collaboration in mind. His idea was that I should help him with a sort of general family history; my interest, however, was principally in the twentieth-century Luxtons and what led up to the tragic deaths on that lonely farm. Somehow I felt that he was unlikely to contact me again.

After my visit to Guildford I immediately wrote to William Luxton inviting him and his wife to visit me at my home in Northamptonshire. I had little hope of receiving an answer, let alone acceptance, but I was wrong. Three days after I wrote he telephoned to say that he would be visiting his son in Birmingham the following weekend and that they would like to stay for one night on the way.

As soon as they got out of the car he opened up the boot and showed me three large cardboard boxes filled with bundles of documents. Incredibly, he had brought everything.

Almost immediately he changed into bedroom slippers and a cardigan. He was keen to get down to work at once and explain everything. I moved back the furniture in my study so that we could spread things about on the floor, and he un-packed his treasures. There were photostats of some three hundred wills, a quantity of ancient farming journals and assorted sheaves of notes pinned together with rusting paper clips, one box of letters and postcards including Frances's letters to William's sisters, and a box of odds and ends includ-ing commonplace books, leather-bound sketch and water-colour books, diaries, school reports, and family history notes written by Frances.

There were also some photographs in an envelope. Until now the Luxtons had only existed for me in my imagination; now I could see what they actually looked like. Robert and Alan were well-scrubbed, bright-eyed looking fellows with open country faces. There was something very appealing and poignant about Frances.

I wanted to delve immediately into the box containing the

letters and the documents in Frances's own hand, but William Luxton restrained me: 'You've got all the time in the world, just let me explain what's here and its significance.'

First, he must show me the family tree. This was a very elaborate affair filling three enormous sheets of paper, each of which could have covered a king-size bed. The names were lovingly copied in minute copperplate – hundreds of them – and he had worked out the relationships back to the seventeenth century in the most elaborate detail. The different branches of the huge family were bewildering and he identified them by referring to the villages and farms of origin: Wembworthy, Bondleigh, Heard's Tenement, Batelease, Brushford Barton, Coldridge, West Chapple.

As the afternoon wore into evening, William Luxton – on all fours and with his back to the log fire, his bald head glistening in the light of the standard lamp – shifted to and fro, to and fro, over the immense family tree. He was obsessed by his family history. He knew every detail of his lineage and was determined that I should share it with him. What impressed me was the sheer time he must have spent: the long days at Somerset House; the weary pilgrimages to damp parish vestries; the arduous eye-strain over census returns, mouldering registers and dusty deeds. He must have known that I was baffled by this game of family Chinese boxes, but he did not seem to care. I had the impression that it pleased him merely to pretend that I was interested. To me it seemed a meaningless rollcall of births, marriages and deaths. I longed for an anecdote, a tangible description, a human reference.

At last, over supper, we returned to flesh and blood and to the Winkleigh Luxtons. William Luxton had pointed out that a great many members of his family had married their first cousins. 'There's probably a good reason for this. You see a man would not go courting beyond an area in which he could ride from his house and back in a day. As they grew in prosperity it must have been increasingly difficult to find suitable partners outside of their own family.'

'Do you think the Winkleigh Luxtons were incestuous?'

'No. Certainly not,' he said with great emphasis.

'Oh, don't you think so?' said his wife at once. Ignoring her husband's disapproving frown, she went on with relish: 'Last time I saw them it certainly crossed my mind that there might be something not quite right about their relationship, if you know what I mean. We often used to visit them on our holidays. It was during the sixties. We were all sitting in the parlour and there was just something about the way they kept exchanging loving glances. It wasn't normal. It was as if they shared a world that nobody else could possibly penetrate.'

'I'm sure there was nothing of that kind in their lives,' Luxton said again, obviously ruffled.

After supper we lingered over a bottle of port and, what with his long drive from Guildford, he was soon ready for bed. As he shuffled up the stairs in his slippers I returned, a little guiltily, to the study and the boxes.

There were two sets of material: the mechanics of William Luxton's family tree, in which I had only a very marginal interest, and the miscellaneous papers from West Chapple Farm, which had been sent down to Guildford by the solicitors in Okehampton. It took very little time to realize that the latter material would answer many questions and fill out the story at West Chapple. The farm journals going back over one hundred years were ancient leather-bound ledgers made by Gutch of Bristol. Browsing through them I got a strong impression of the daily round of work and the variety of farming activities. Against each day's date there were dozens of entries. Every minor detail of cattle- and sheep-breeding was logged, cows and calves being mentioned by name and ewes and rams by individual markings. There were detailed accounts of all dairy produce down to the last egg and half pint of milk. There were records of every row of potatoes, faggot of wood and trapped rabbit, all in old-fashioned copperplate. Some of the pages were devoted to accumulating information – such as labourers' holidays. I was astonished to learn that even in recent times Fred Lyne would lose a day's holiday if he were sent home because of bad weather. Here was Fred Lyne's 'Holiday Account' for the year 1969. Fred had not exaggerated about losing time when he was out bell-ringing:

April 20th.   ½ day J. Saunders funeral.
May 8th.   ½ day J. Knight funeral.
June 18th.   1 day wedding ringing.
July 28, 29, 30, 31, August 1st, 2nd.   6 days holiday.
October 13 and 14th.   Home ill.
November 25th.   1 day home.   Very bad weather.
December 5th.   1 day Exeter about glasses.

By the side of these entries the writer (I presumed it was Robbie Luxton) had written 'one day owing in 1969'.

There were dozens of quaint prescriptions, cures and recipes, all copied out with loving care in very large copperplate: 'To kill sting nettles cut them 2 or 3 years in succession on the 24th of May, June and July.' Or 'In treating a bad cold a cooling cleansing, germ-destroying laxative such as Karmoid Tablets should be taken at once. About 2 tablets, with half a glass of water is the average dose.' There were instructions for pruning and grafting, prescriptions for sheep dips, recommendations for the destruction of wasps' nests.

There was little of narrative interest in the farm journals, so I turned to the letters, postcards and commonplace books with mounting excitement. At a guess, there appeared to be some three thousand letters and postcards, some in large brown envelopes, others tied in bundles and in no particular order. Initially I found them disappointing. They dated from the 1870s and all related to the Luxtons of Winkleigh. Many of them were banal messages from people I had no way of identifying. There were hand-delivered notes from labourers such as this in 1892:

Dear Sir,

    am sorry am not feeling well enough
    for work to day if I go to bed to day
    shall be quite allright tomorrow.   D. Jarvis.

Or this mystifying note in the same hand and in the same year:

Dear Sir I am sorry I cannot come to work to day
I have the horse wheel of Pound out of its Place at
Stabdon hope to come tomorrow.

    Wilmot Luxton (*née* Short), Frances Luxton's mother, had seemed to me a shadowy figure in my interviews. I was intrigued to discover that she had brought her parents' correspondence with her to West Chapple after her marriage. I found her letters home from a girls' boarding school in Chulmleigh in a little bundle tied with fading purple ribbon. Here is a typical example dated 11 April 1898, the handwriting as stiff as the prose:

My dear Parents,

    Miss Powlerland wishes me to inform you that our Vacation will (D.V.) commence on Thursday next, when I hope to have the pleasure of seeing you again.
    I trust you will be satisfied with the progress I have endeavoured to make in my various studies. Our Examination is over and prizes are to be distributed tomorrow. Miss Powlerland desires her kindest regards to you each, and with love from myself,

                    I remain,
                    Your loving daughter
                    Wilmot

In the midst of this rigid little bundle I came upon a letter to Wilmot's parents from Miss Powlerland herself. She says: 'I have found Wilmot a dear girl – always ready to please her teachers and to obey the rules – if you know of any others to go away to school may I ask you for your kind interest and recommendation?'

At length I came upon a series of letters from Frances herself to her parents in 1938. They appeared to be written from Scotland and the headed notepaper bore the title Cooperative Holidays Association. There was a series of postcards and letters from Frances to her brothers in 1967, written from Italy, Malta, Israel and Rhodes, and clearly the product of her visit to the Holy Land. They were, in fact, routine holiday correspondence, and at first sight fairly unremarkable. This sort of thing, dated 5 April 1967: 'Am still at sea after two days sailing since left Malta very calm and warm sunshine ship rolls gently but have not been sick, but lots of others have, this is an Italian ship the Mt Olympus ran aground last week.'

Then I opened a brown envelope and out fell a huge package of letters and postcards, at least three hundred of them, all written in the same tiny, neat hand and spanning the years 1950–54. They were signed R, and eventually I found on the back of an envelope the correspondent's full name – R. Wagemaker – and an address in Haarlem, Holland. Many of the letters were written from Haarlem, but others came from ports all over the world – Curaçao, Santos, Copenhagen, Piraeus, Liverpool, Cape Town ... At the beginning of each letter or postcard he consistently thanked her for having written to him earlier before leading into his oddly phrased communications: for example, this, dated 7 June 1950:

Dearest Frances,

I beg to thank you again for your p.c. recently received. What boisterous summer weather, we are enjoying. May be it makes us

strong and healthy. Some people maintain this extraordinary cold
and wet is a result of big changes in the Arctic atmosphere. Perhaps?
Am keeping pretty fit, but not too gay. Want to travel and go abroad
again soon. Best wishes to you dear Frances. And let diplomats and
politicians go on trying to create peace on earth.

He would go on for thousands of words in this stilted,
impersonal vein, but every so often there would be a flash of
personal engagement such as in this of 12 April 1951:

My dearest Frances,

At last a little sunshine. Let the sodden soil get a little dry and start
sowing the seeds for next crop. The bulbs are late with us, but will
flower all the same. They seem to be able to stand the cold. My
youngest daughter Reina registered to marry yesterday. The wedding will take place on Friday 4th May, the day after Ascension, they
say. As we live in critical hard times, according to our finance
minister, the ceremony will be held in a sober way.

The winter in Holland has been catastrophal for farmers and
townsplaces. I had a housekeeper three months long, but could not
keep her. Disbehaving in many ways. Now I lead a wandering life
and take meals outdoors. I hope to meet you again this summer if I
come to England. Perhaps we will meet if I visit Gwen.

How are you dear Frances? Are you also so glad that winter did
not reign long and spring is announcing her arrival now? I should
like to travel more but alas my services are not wanted anymore.
Younger people step in now. So long Fr, be good and write. Yours
R.W.

What was a Dutch seaman doing corresponding with
Frances, who was supposed to have been a recluse much of her
life? How and when had they met? And who was Gwen?

I returned the letters to their stout brown envelope and
picked up one of the commonplace books. It had been kept by
Frances in childhood, possibly to the age of fourteen or fifteen.
There were pretty watercolours of country scenes, woods and

fields and sunsets; quotations from nineteenth-century poems
and from the Bible; proverbs and aphorisms:

> Worldly pleasures
> Take them while you may
> The mill will never grind
> With the waters of yesterday

On several pieces of paper she had copied out neatly the
following verse, which seemed to be an epitaph. Had she
composed it, intending it for her own headstone? Or had she
copied it from an existing grave?

> As you pass on see here where I lie
> While living some did me deny
> In hope God will receive my Soul
> Thro Jesus Christ who died for all,
> False witness did rise up
> They laid to my charge
> Things that I knew not
> They rewarded me evil for good
> To the great discomfort of my soul.

As I worked my way through the odd jumble of family
memorabilia, no single item offered a satisfying portion of
narrative; yet I knew that here were abundant clues to the
Luxtons' story, essential parts of the jigsaw.

In an envelope I found evidence of Frances's attempts to
gather the family history. There were hundreds of miscellaneous notes, written on odd scraps of notepaper, children's
exercise books, the backs of white paper bags and the insides
of broken cigarette packets.

Disappointingly they were simply notes and no more: from
one scrap of paper I transcribed this typical item:

Great Grandfather Luxton lived at Winkleigh Court from 1822–
1834 and six of his eight children were baptized in Winkleigh

Church. Date of baptism John 8th Jan 1823, Robert 18 Sept 1825. William received into the congregation 15 Nov 1828. Lawrence 14 Jan 1829. Charity Ann 1st April 1831. Frances Sarah 15 March 1843. This can be seen in the register of Winkleigh Church – Great Grandfather farmed Winkleigh Court at the time.

Many of the paper scraps merely recorded what she had copied from gravestones. Curiously, I found that some of the information was repeated over and over again. It certainly explained how she came to haunt the graveyards of Winkleigh and Brushford. Reading through these gravestone transcriptions I got an impression of the same sort of obsession as I found in William Luxton. What compelled them both to press ever further back through the forest of names and dates? What did they hope to find, or to achieve? And in the case of Frances, to whom had she meant to pass on the information?

My head reeling, I finally went to bed at three o'clock and slept badly.

Bill Luxton was up early the next morning and eager to get back to the family history. Over breakfast I asked quite casually who R. Wagemaker was, and how he had come to meet Frances. And who was Gwen? For a moment he looked stunned.

'I see you've been at the other stuff,' he said with obvious disapproval. 'Oh well, I can't blame you. I suppose it's more interesting to you than my dry old family tree. Gwen, in fact, is my sister. There's no great mystery. I have two sisters – Kate and Gwen; they lived for many years in Highbury. Frances came there once when she was a small child and liked them enormously. They were both older than Frances and being townsfolk a lot more sophisticated. Kate was born in 1902 at exactly the same moment, to the second, that Queen Victoria died. Gwen was born in 1904. On several occasions during her life Frances simply disappeared from Winkleigh and turned up on their doorstep without any warning. Once or twice she found them away from home and went straight back to Devon. I'm not sure how Wagemaker met my sister, but he was a Dutch sea captain. He was very short with a large bulldog head and great hanging jowls like Churchill. When war broke out his ship was in Liverpool and, like all British shipping out of Holland, it came under British control. He became some sort of consultant to the Admiralty for the rest of the war, as he spoke fairly good English. He was a widower and lonely, and after he met Gwen he proposed to her. She turned him down. She told me, "I didn't think of him like that." Although marriage wasn't on the cards he continued to write to Gwen and to visit her after the war, and she went over to Holland for a holiday. I think his daughter looked after him. Well, one year – it must have been towards the end of the forties – he was on one of his infrequent trips to London and visiting Highbury when Frances turned up unexpectedly. Wage-maker fell for her in a big way and they never stopped talking. Frances was always interested in travel and she had a romantic idea about going to sea. They sat in the drawing room and Frances listened to Wagemaker's life story with her eyes standing out of her head – he'd been at sea for forty years by this stage. I gathered at the time that he was interested in her, but I had no idea that they corresponded in this way. It would be fascinating to know what Frances found to tell him about Winkleigh. I knew that they had struck up some sort of friendship, but I think he must have felt embarrassed by his earlier proposal to Gwen. He continued to show a lot of interest in Gwen throughout the rest of his life, but I think he had transferred his affections to Frances. I must say that my sister would probably be shocked and rather upset to know that Wage-maker had also been interested in Frances. Of course, he's been dead some years now.'

Back in the study I continued to ply William Luxton with

questions about the small section of the family in which I was interested, and at last he began to open up and talk, with just an occasional bleak look at the family tree lying out in the centre of the carpet. As he talked, a sketchy picture began to emerge of a huge and prosperous family breaking up and scattering to the four quarters of the globe in the space of one generation. 'I can't tell you how significant that break-up must have been. When I was a boy visiting West Chapple for the first time on my bicycle from Exeter, I called at Inch's cider factory and asked for the Luxton farm; an old man in there said to me, "This used to be Luxton country round here – all of it for miles and miles in every direction."'

What seemed curious to me was that William and Frances Luxton had both been obsessed with the idea of simply recording the extent of this enormous family in all its complicated detail, with no apparent interest in the reasons for its break-up and dissolution. For Frances, the need to put her forebears in touch with each other on paper seemed to have become an all-embracing mission as she faced the stark fact that she and her brothers were the last surviving Luxtons in Winkleigh. And the closer she got to leaving West Chapple Farm, the more intensively and the more chaotically she worked. It was as if she felt that she owed some appalling debt to all those Luxtons filling the churchyards of dozens of surrounding parishes; and as if the hundreds of cousins and aunts and uncles who had scattered to the ends of the earth had bequeathed her the burden of being keeper of the family's conscience, keeper of the family's memories and ghosts.

William Luxton was convinced that the Winkleigh Luxtons, by escaping the fate that had struck the rest of the family, had become strangely fossilized. At last he began to talk about the real Luxtons that were his flesh and blood. We must have talked for five or six hours, not even breaking for lunch. He was in possession of an enormous circuit of family lore, none of it written. It became clear that the turning point in the Luxton fortunes had been the great farming depression of the late nineteenth century that wiped out tens of thousands of farms in Britain and drove hundreds of thousands of farmers and their labourers overseas. Somehow, alone of the Luxtons, the Winkleigh family had survived the general disaster. William Luxton pointed out that the miserliness, the seclusion, the determination to stick to old methods, were probably their only means of survival: 'They just shut the gate and shut out the world and said, "All right, so we can't make money out of farming, but we'll feed ourselves and spend nothing." The extraordinary thing is that they went on doing it for two more generations.'

After tea the Luxtons had to leave for Birmingham. William Luxton said solemnly, 'I'm leaving these things in your charge. I wish you well with your book. But I do think you should seriously consider leaving the Winkleigh Luxtons out of it altogether.'

'I'm not sure what sort of book I'll write,' I said with a fair degree of honesty.

A Family History

The Luxtons were proud and physically strong, with high fore-heads, broad shoulders and steady blue eyes. They were also moody, quick to anger and deeply religious. In the fourteenth century there was a Robert Luggesdon, yeoman, living in the ancient homestead of Lutehouse in Chapple Valley west of Winkleigh. From his line the clan spread out, through the neighbouring districts of Brushford, Witheridge, Wembworthy, Coldridge and Eggesford, until by the early nineteenth century the greater family owned a hundred farms spread over several thousand acres between Exmoor and Dartmoor. In the eighteenth century each son could expect to inherit a farm intact with tithe cottages and other properties. Daughters and widowed aunts could expect annuities from properties in Exeter, Plymouth and Okehampton.

At the climax of the family fortunes in the mid nineteenth century the undisputed head of the Winkleigh clan was Robert George Luxton, 'Maister' of Brushford Barton, with ten servants, a pack of fox hounds and a stable full of hunters. Robert George had inherited six farms comprising some 2,000 acres, together with stock, numerous cottages and a consider-able fortune in furnishings, pictures, silver, delft and glass-ware. He had £3,000 in the bank. The future looked pros-perous for Robert George. He was born in 1818 and grew up in a rural society in which most of the values and rituals of the eighteenth century seemed unalterable. Although his wealth had been based on the strict husbandry and shrewdness of small yeoman farmers, he now affected the tastes and arrogance of the country aristocracy and took to racing, foxhunting, heavy drink and gambling.

In all this he had a mentor and close crony in the Fifth Earl of Portsmouth. The traveller on the road from Exeter to Barnstaple can see the sad ruin of the Earl's house high on a hill above Eggesford. It was once the centre of a great estate which involved a considerable proportion of the economy of North Devon. To this day locals of Eggesford attempt to impress visitors with yarns about the Earl's household. Portsmouth had built the mansion in 1854 as an act of conscious extravagance. It was a modish, gothic affair with pinnacles and all sorts of 'foreign' frippery. There were six lofty and gorgeously decorated reception rooms, each big enough to hold a ball; thirty magnificent bedrooms for guests, each with its own commodious dressing room and bathroom, and as many servants' rooms. Like some island hotel, the establishment was completely self-sufficient, with laundries, dairies, bakeries, and workshops, a forge, kitchen gardens covering dozens of acres and stabling for fifty fine horses. The main carriage drive to the mansion was one mile long and there were seven miles of private walks through ornamental gardens. A team of staff working shifts was fully occupied in attending the forests of candles and thousands of lamps. There were twenty gardeners producing all manner of exotic flowers and every kind of fruit and vegetable; their produce was borne up to the house in panniers by donkeys.

In the season there was hunting every day and at the end of the day's run the company sat down to a gargantuan dinner, the consumption of which was in itself a notable feat. The Earl exercised almost feudal rights, dispensing justice in the main hall seated in an enormous chair made from an elm tree grown on the estate and carved with perfect precision to fit his vast backside in tight riding breeches. The feet of his chair were mounted on the hooves of a favourite hunter.

When the Exeter to Barnstaple railway with its unsightly telegraph poles and tunnels was driven through his estate in the 1850s, he reserved the right to stop any train – including the express – for the convenience of himself and, of course, his guests.

With his access to men of business and science in London, including the famous James Caird, high priest of 'high farming', Portsmouth was persuaded to spend freely from his vast resources on agricultural improvements and he prevailed on Robert George to follow suit. The economists were saying that a depression lay ahead, and that only those who laid careful plans and went for high productivity would be able to survive the inevitable slump. 'High farming' was simply intensive farming. It meant laying down huge quantities of fertilizer to produce the highest possible yield; it meant using the best available seed and breeding the finest livestock on the smallest possible acreage. The policy was valid, of course, only so long as markets kept expanding, prices remained high and labour remained cheap. Robert George invested in steam power for threshing and ploughing, artificial manure and extensive drainage schemes. He attempted to double his crop yield and treble his stock. To improve his dairy produce he purchased a patent milking machine from the United States – efficient, speedy and labour-saving. Having spent some £8 an acre improving his soil he thought it only prudent to improve his yards, barns and sheds. Brick-built dairies, cow pens and pigsties were erected at Brushford, along with Dutch barns to receive the increase in crops.

Through Portsmouth's influence Robert George became Master of the Eggesford Hunt and the toast of the hunting fraternity of North Devon. Keeping a pack of foxhounds in the mid nineteenth century cost not less than £500 a year, and to hunt with conviction, as Robert George certainly did, could cost more than £2,000 a year.

In the 1860s and 1870s Robert George financed his enormous investments and other extravagances from loans, which the bank directors in Okehampton and Exeter were only too pleased to provide on short term at seven per cent. His farms became the basis of his credit, and so did his crops, his thoroughbred horses and his stock. At the same time he became a familiar face at Tattersall's and at the races. There were reckless private bets among Lord Portsmouth's party at point-to-points.

His sons went to Blundell's School and disdained to work with their hands; his daughters preferred lounging with novels to helping out in the dairy as their mother and grandmothers had done in their youth. All summer long the children whooped and disported themselves on the new lawn tennis court. In winter they were out with guns and dogs when they weren't riding to hounds. Growing distant from his men, Robert George became less capable of controlling them. He went to bed late (invariably drunk) and rose late, hung over. In the interval between breakfast and the hunting field he had little opportunity to issue decisive orders, and he had no system for checking that the orders had been fulfilled.

Next to his passion for horses (he had his right eye kicked out by a favourite hunter at forty years of age) was his passion for women, especially his cousins and the wives of his cousins. Himself the child of first cousins (his father had married a cousin named Laetitia Luxton), Robert George was to marry, in turn, his cousin Amelia Luxton of Winkleigh (who died ten years later after giving him a son and a daughter), then another cousin, Susan Luxton, who was both the widow of one of Robert George's cousins and a daughter of two Luxton cousins. To cap it all, Robert George's grandparents had also been cousins.

He showered his womenfolk with gifts, and as head of the clan paid out pensions to relatives in every quarter of Devon as a necessary consequence of his complex inheritance. Not surprisingly the gossip spread throughout Devon, in the ale houses and auction rooms. 'Where do the money come from, eh? Tha's riding for a fall, for sure. I remember his father driving cows in a smock.'

But of all his critics none was more scathing than his first cousin Lawrence Luxton of West Chapple, Winkleigh. Lawrence and Robert George were much of an age; they had grown up together, measured each other's strengths and weaknesses in youth. But although their farms were a mere hour's walking distance apart, a coldness developed between them after they came into their inheritances. By comparison with Robert George, Lawrence was a poor small-time farmer. Lawrence saw his cousin mixing with 'the county', he observed his spendthrift farming, he noticed with contempt his drinking and gambling. He predicted catastrophe.

The catastrophe, when it came, was more widespread and appalling and permanent than any could have guessed. The background to the agricultural depression of the latter half of the nineteenth century was the influx of cheap food from the United States, Russia, Argentina, Australia and New Zealand. Steam navigation and the relentlessly spreading tentacles of the railways in every part of the world brought speedier, cheaper transport. The Americans had pioneered the mechanization of crop farming on an unparalleled scale to open up and exploit the vast and fertile prairies. Inevitably the food markets of the world were transformed. It was an era of aggressive free trade and British farming was brought to the edge of collapse. Throughout the 1870s North American grain pushed prices down to levels unknown since before the year 1700. The populations of the manufacturing towns were being fed on Argentine beef, Australian mutton and bread made with American wheat. In the 1880s the cost of a loaf fell to half its previous price. Denmark counteracted the changing market forces by rapidly switching to dairy produce. The

Danish farmer fed cheap imported grain to dairy cattle and pigs, and exported high-quality standardized bacon to England.

Many British crop farmers converted their farms to grassland, hoping to redeem their fortunes by investing in milk production. As a result there were huge milk surpluses and plummeting prices meant they failed to cover their investments. Their attempts to break into the cheese markets were frustrated as they watched American cheese drop to twopence a pound. No British farmer could produce good cheese for less than fourpence a pound.

Attempts to diversify were not helped by a series of appalling seasons during the early years of the depression. Then in 1879 it simply rained without ceasing throughout the whole of the summer, turning much of the English countryside into a desperate, oozing mire. It continued to rain until the end of 1882, causing an epidemic of pleuro-pneumonia and liver rot in sheep, while the crops collapsed in the fields. The middle of the decade was marked by severe droughts and catastrophic frosts. S. G. Kendall, the West Country yeoman farmer who kept a detailed diary of the weather, vividly describes the year 1879 and the following five years of appalling summers. The persistent rain that summer, he wrote, was accompanied 'by a damp, dark, cold atmosphere which struck a chill almost into one's bones, bringing ruined crops with widespread devastation in their train ... We had no barley crops at all that season on heavy soil', and the wheat 'turned blighty and black and seemed to shrink back in a different way yet not dissimilar to the barley two months earlier'.

Another diarist, George Rope, describes the floods that summer: '23 Aug. Began cutting tolavera – slightly sprouted as it stood – from continual rains for the last fortnight. The wettest season since 1860 and similar, but not so cold – about two-thirds of the hay and clover spoiled – and a large quantity carried away by floods – on 22nd July we had the greatest flood I can ever remember.' He goes on to describe cows drowned, houses flooded, and how people had travelled by boat from farm to farm.

At the end of 1879 Kendall wrote: 'This dismal, wet, dark, never-to-be-forgotten year is now at an end; may the coming eighties bring with it better luck and greater good fortune.' But 1880 was if anything worse – bad weather and disease carried away five million sheep in England; and 1881 brought fresh disasters including a blizzard lasting forty-eight hours. G. E. Mingay, who has chronicled the weather during this period in his *Rural Life in Victorian England*, summarizes the continued disastrous weather thus:

The following summer was wet, and 1882 had a very wet autumn so that little wheat could be sown. The summers of 1885 and 1887, by contrast, were dry, with shortages of roots for the stock ... the early nineties saw fresh disasters. The great blizzard of 8–13 March 1891 brought twenty-foot snow drifts to parts of the West Country, and claimed over 200 lives on shore and at sea. The farmers suffered great losses of livestock – some sheep were blown over the cliffs into the sea – as well as devastation in orchards and woodlands. The summer of 1891 also produced a wet harvest, and 1892 and 1893 brought very severe droughts. In [the West Country] hardly any rain fell between February and July 1893, and there was almost no grass for haymaking. On the heavy land the harrow marks of April could be seen right up to harvest. Then came a most bitter and persistent frost in the winter of 1894–5, when drifts of snow from six to fourteen feet deep covered the ground for weeks.

Thousands of farmers were wiped out and abandoned farming for good. Many sold up and emigrated to the colonies. As William Wordsworth put it, describing a similar depression at the turn of the previous century, 'many rich were sunk down as in a dream amongst the poor'.

Throughout the seventies Robert George's harvests rotted

in the fields while the gangs of men who had been paid in hard cash played cards and drank his cider under the dripping eaves of the new sheds. The men had to be kept on in case the deluge stopped and the hay could be brought in. Meanwhile those expensively purchased haymaking machines and elevators lay rusting while Robert George contemplated the likely cost of feed for the winter.

In the end he was forced to start selling off his land and assets piecemeal and at knockdown prices. In the meantime many of his less fortunate relatives, who in normal times might have looked to him for assistance, sold up completely and emigrated. It was a familiar pattern throughout England in those harsh days. Between 1870 and the turn of the century 700,000 farmers and farmworkers emigrated.

Luxtons settled in Colorado, Los Angeles, San Francisco, Vancouver, Toronto, Christchurch in New Zealand, Cape Town and Sydney. Some travelled shorter distances. Canon Girdlestone of Halberton in North Devon helped organize the migration of destitute families from his locality to the industrial towns in the north. He sent them off labelled like parcels, and reported that many of them had never travelled further than a few miles from their cottages in their entire lives and thought that Manchester lay across the sea.

John Luxton of Bondleigh ran off to Exeter to become a butcher's boy, then walked to London, where he founded a prosperous engineering firm. One of his sons, William (the Guildford Luxton), passed through Banff on a business trip to Canada in 1963, and found a sign up announcing 'Luxton Museum'. It was a collection of Indian crafts collected by Norman Luxton, who had left Winkleigh in the nineties and had lived at first by bartering pelts for tobacco. He was now eighty years of age. When William introduced himself and tried to initiate a conversation about Winkleigh, the old man yelled at him: 'Get out of here! I'm not interested; I don't want to know about my family.' William Luxton wonders to this day whether Norman was frightened that he would ask for money, or whether there were other, more poignant, reasons.

The break-up and dissolution of Robert George's inheritance continued for over a quarter of a century until he was left with nothing but the empty house at Brushford. But still he rode to hounds and with him his two sons by his second marriage to his cousin's widow. Robert George finally broke his neck in a hunting accident and died in 1902 aged 84. He left an empty and mortgaged house and £30 to cover funeral expenses. His crony, the Earl of Portsmouth, died in 1906, having taken his own life.

Robert George's younger son, Augustus, went on hunting in a threadbare coat and leaking boots until his death in 1922. He died of a heart attack in a room above the kennels which he shared with the whipper-in of the Eggesford pack, John Taylor Lyne, a cousin of Fred Lyne of Winkleigh. Robert George's eldest son, Alfred Morgan, lived to a great age and died in 1946 in a terraced house in Station Road, Budleigh Salterton.

The story of the Winkleigh Luxtons in the latter part of the nineteenth century is one of unrelieved decline and break-up. But despite the bankrupts, the emigrants and the failures, Lawrence Luxton of West Chapple was determined not only to stay, but to survive and thrive. Lawrence and Mary Luxton had two daughters, Fanny and Mary Louisa, and one son, Robert John, born in 1870. Lawrence set about bringing up Robert John with the right attitudes towards farming and life. At his father's knee Robert John learned about the depression as it unfolded, and he had daily lessons about the folly of his uncle Robert George.

Lawrence taught Robert John about the pressure of market forces, the mania for new-fangled methods of improving productivity, the practice of borrowing huge loans for improvement on the security of notional stock and crops and at rocketing interest rates. He pointed out the example of his relatives and neighbours and he concluded that the real evil was growth and speed and expenditure. Take the modern notion of beef, he would say: the system was to fatten as much stock as the farmer could put on his acreage as fast as possible and to sell on as fast as possible. Thus a farmer would buy cattle on speculation and feed on expensive cake. He would take risks beyond his resources and gamble his very birthright year after year.

On the other hand, thought Lawrence, a farmer who was prepared to wait could breed from his own stock and fatten them on hay from his own fields. True, they would go down to nothing in a hard winter, but the secret was to strike the perfect balance between the size of herd and the extent and quality of acreage. In a good summer they would fatten up beautifully and he would sell in the autumn if the market was right. And what if things got even worse than they were at present? What if beef prices slumped even further? With no expenditure one could at least survive and make a small profit. And if the worst came to the worst, he argued, one could simply operate a system of self-sufficiency: he had land, he had water, he had woods and orchards, he had a modest investment in stock. Well then, why not just shut the gate and survive till better days came?

The more Lawrence contemplated the matter the more he grew enamoured, indeed obsessed, with the idea of independence from the forces that had driven so many of his neighbours and relatives from the land. The problem was not with farming, it was not even with the American prairies, or Danish bacon, or repeal of the Corn Laws. The problem was allowing one's farming economy to be influenced by these outside forces. It was said that a hard-working man and his family could survive on four acres and a cow. Well, here he was with 230 acres, mostly facing south, with streams and woods, a sturdy flock of ewes and a herd of beautiful cows specially chosen for their fine breeding qualities. He had a productive kitchen garden and orchard. He made cider and stored sweet apples for the winter. His wife was practised in all the arts of farmhouse economy and he himself was capable of working alongside his labourers in the fields. He had a sturdy son who had worked as a labourer, strong daughters who would work as hard as their mother. He paid his labourers as much as possible in kind and kept a strict record of everything they consumed. They looked to him for their milk, wood for fuel, vegetables and cider, and Mrs Luxton supplied bread, cheese and butter. They lived in his cottages and fed on his potatoes. Everything was measured, everything was reckoned up; for if he was to practise a true barter economy then every penny spent was a crime against the virtue of true self-sufficiency.

He could encourage neither neighbours nor relatives in social contact, for that meant expenditure. He would give to the church a percentage of his meagre profits, since, just as one gave back to the land what one took from it, God must be accorded his due for having brought him good fortune. That, after all, was only good husbandry. And whereas even the poorest of his relations, not to mention Robert George, had kept open and generous house, Lawrence would entertain nobody – unless, of course, they paid. Occasionally he had two agricultural students, and there were nephews and nieces who stayed from time to time. But these were strict business arrangements that supplied much-needed spare cash for those few necessities like clothes and boots that could not be secured by barter.

The family lived more harshly than their guests, and indeed even more harshly than their own labourers. When there were paying guests just one joint of mutton would be supplied and it would last the rest of the week. But Lawrence and the family would be content with the coarse and fatty bacon that had been cured in the brine bath in the kitchen.

Any spare money was put carefully into bonds or kept in cash in the house safe. When he bought new stock it was generally cheap and out of condition. He bought a second-hand reaping machine to save money on labour and it was kept in service well into the twentieth century. He kept a fine brood mare that did its fair share of farm work and was put regularly to horse. With luck a colt born in the spring could be sold for £30 in the autumn. He got around the farm on horseback throughout the day, keeping an eye on his labourers' progress and how everything stood.

Lawrence never shot except crows and other vermin, but he trapped rabbits and sold them for cash in Winkleigh. He sold moleskins; he ran a sheep-dip business for his neighbours; he rented out his water-driven threshing and crushing machines for cash. He had no fancy drainage systems in mind, no schemes for new barns or sheds. His tools and implements were kept in excellent order, cleaned and greased and properly hung at the end of each day. Many of them would still be in excellent condition a century later.

Lawrence's wife Mary died in 1889 and he himself died in 1892. Robert John became the 'Maister' while the cumulative effects of the depression were still destroying farms up and down the country. Throughout his twenties Robert John laboured as his father had done before him. Mary Louisa married Arthur Knapman and moved down to Okehampton, Fanny lived at West Chapple until the late nineties when she married a man called George Raymont and moved to St Audries. Then in 1906 Robert John married a dark-eyed local beauty, Wilmot Summerhayes Short. She came from provident yeoman farming stock and her parents had made great sacrifices to send her to a private school in Chulmleigh; they thought she had done well to become mistress of West Chapple, to which she brought a small settlement in the form of an income from a rented cottage in Winkleigh.

Two years later when Robert John Luxton learned that Wilmot had given birth to a daughter he was keenly disappointed. Not only was a girl useless for heavy work on the land, she would eventually meet a young man and probably marry – demanding a dowry – before any future sons could increase his meagre substance.

Frances was a strong, red-headed, pale-skinned Luxton. She grew up against the background of her father's brooding disappointment and the rigorous discipline of his farm and household. There were, after all, to be sons – Robbie came in 1911 and then Alan ten years later. But her father never resigned himself to the bad luck of having a daughter for his first-born and seemed determined to exact some form of compensation.

Frances grew up to daily stories of family dissolution and lost fortunes. Nightly at the supper table she was harangued about irreligion, bad husbandry, crop failure, distemper, bad marriages, incest and debt. Daily, in one form or another, he inculcated the Luxton philosophy: 'You cannot take out more than you put in.'

Her mother, Wilmot Summerhayes, never ceased to remind Robert John that she had brought substance to West Chapple Farm. She had paid her way. She did not think it unusual that her husband should discourse on giving and taking when he spoke of the soil, but she nursed her own resentments – principally, that she had aspired to be a lady, to have status in the community by her association with the Luxton family. She discovered too late that Robert regarded all social intercourse as unproductive, wasteful and dangerous. The only outside contact he would admit was church-going: this was fully

consistent with his strict view of life. One gave God one's due
in prayer and tithes and he would reward in due measure.

The daily round at West Chapple was in part dictated by
the seasons of the year, but there was a consistent and unvary-
ing pattern of work from which none was excused. Robert
John was a yeoman farmer as he never tired of telling his family,
and this indicated that he was a small but proud independent
farmer: he neither worked for another man, as would a mere
tenant, nor employed others to do what he could do himself.
Thus he worked alongside his labourers and he expected his
daughter to work alongside her mother – in the house, in the
dairy and in the orchard and vegetable garden.

The day began at a quarter to six when she heard her father
clattering in his heavy boots down the narrow stairs and
straight out into the yard. Her mother would call her several
minutes later and the round of kitchen-cleaning, fire-lighting
and stove-minding would start. A breakfast of tea and coarse
bread preceded by prayers was at 7.30, followed by the main
work of the day, unless Frances was due to go to school, which
was seldom – particularly in the busy months from April to the
end of September.

Frances also helped from her earliest years with the making
of cider and thick Devon clotted cream. The Luxtons patiently
waited for the natural falling of the cider apples from their
orchard at the side of the house. The huge press was in a dry
and spacious outhouse where there was a room known simply
as the apple-store in which the fruit was collected and allowed
to undergo its first sweating. Robert John had notes in a book
passed down from generation to generation:

The vessels being all well cleansed and scalded, are filled with
cider from the press, which in a day or two begins to work, throwing
off large quantities of dregs and impurities of the liquor; this will
sometimes subside to the bottom, but whether it sinks or issues from
the bung-hole, as the weather may be more or less warm, it will

require racking from time to time, to separate the dregs from the liquor.

The cider was not for the benefit of the family at West Chapple, but formed part of the farmworkers' pay. Every quart was strictly measured and deducted from their wages. Any cider left over would be sold to a dealer from London who called in March and paid cash after a sampling ceremony.

The Luxtons kept a small herd of cows that were a cross between North Devon and Old Marlborough Red. Robert John believed that the pure outdoor air produced better milk, so the herd was seldom sheltered except in the very worst weeks of winter. The animals were known by names which had been passed down through the ages like the names of the fields they grazed: Star, Beauty, Short Horn, Longlegs, One Eye, Dark, Sparky, Stumpy. The Luxtons' fields were known by such names as Chubhouse Orchard, Blindwells, Lower Ley, Chapple Meadow, Garden Close and Chapple Down. Few were more than ten acres.

From early childhood Frances was taught how to make cheese, butter and cream in the dairy, which was part of the main farmhouse directly adjoining the kitchen. There in the dark rancid air she worked with her mother, often by lantern light.

The milk was put into earthen vessels holding about twelve quarts each to stand for half a day, or through the night, and then poured into a broad iron pan and heated over a stove until the whole body of cream formed upon the surface. This was gently removed by the edge of a ladle into a churn and there stirred by hand with a stick about a foot long. During this process some twelve pounds of cream was separated from the buttermilk at a time: this was the celebrated Devonshire clotted, or clouted, cream.

Robert John would come in from the fields or the yard at

twelve o'clock for his dinner, and there would be talk of the stock. After eating soup and bread and a dish of potatoes, green vegetables in season and cold meat from the Sunday joint, or cured bacon, he would clear a space on the table and do his 'paperwork' in a ledger. The Luxton ledgers were traditional eighteenth-century notebooks, stocks of which survived down to the last day of the Luxtons' lives. They were used to record the events that could not be committed to memory, and in the mind of the senior Luxton would have constituted the letter of the law when it came to rents and payments. Here are some random records from one year between the wars.

Jan 10	D. Jarvis had 225 + 10 of wood + 15 more = 250 faggots.
Jan 27	S. Marrin had 37 sacks of wheat 14/2 per cwt.
March 12	W. Knight had one sheep.
March 15	All calves injected for felon except two sucking heifers.
March 30	Sold wool to J. Cole 108 fleeces at 1/3 per lb.
April 1	A. Wanacott had half pig.
April 7	Star's calf born (bull calf).
April 14	Potatoes: 10 drills King Georges. Great Scots next. Field Marshalls next. Kerrs Pinks next. Majestic in corner.
May 9	Sold fat barrener to S. Lendon had 1 calf.
May 19	Tidy went to horse.
June 24	J. Mitchell hay harvest overtime: 8th two hours 10th ¾ hour 12th 3½ at 1/- an hour.
July 1	No of sheep dipped 260.
August 4	Blossom went to horse June 26th returned today.
August 22	Ram went with old ewes Aug 22nd. Young Ram went with young ewes. Aug 22nd 4 ewes went to young ram first fortnight right shoulder.
	PAID.
August 14	I had nail boots size 6 price 25/-.

Sept 9   D. Jarvis Rent 7/6.

Oct 4   J. Hooper went for holiday comes back Oct 11th.

Nov   R. M. Chambers rabbit account. Started trapping
             Nov 24th Nov 25th and 26th 60 27th 28th 29th 62
             and 14 damaged by dogs.

Dec 22   Bull calf. A.Wanacott put to Up Horn £4.17/6.

Dec 27   Mrs S. Dunn ground 26 bushels of grain.

In her childhood dolls and dolls' houses and similar play-things were unknown to Frances. Almost as soon as she could talk Wilmot taught Frances to read and write and she began to keep a commonplace book of notes, quotations, drawings and pressed flowers. This is where she indulged her eager imagination. But there was little time for such pursuits during the day; if she was not engaged in some duty there was always Robbie, her younger brother, to look after. He was three years younger – a stolid silent little boy much given to staring hard, who clung to her devotedly as she took him through the yard to feed the chickens or down the lane to pick wild flowers.

In the late afternoon there was tea, the third and last meal of the day, at about six o'clock. This normally consisted of bread and a piece of cheese, with lettuce or a tomato in summer, and a piece of cake.

When he had finished, Robert John would always reach down his Bible and read a favourite passage at table before going out again to the yard.

Frances's reading was restricted to the books which were kept in the house – lugubrious-looking tomes of Milton, Bunyan, Tennyson, Shakespeare, and a number of works of theology and religious devotion. Novels, newspapers and magazines were never purchased. Not only would Robert John have disapproved of the expense, he would never have approved of the vain sentiments and dubious morals expressed in such trivia. Thus Frances grew up with only scanty and strange notions of the world outside West Chapple. Of the country beyond Mid-Devon she had only the very vaguest idea, and of foreign countries she had little knowledge except from the images provided by the huge oleographs of the Holy Land she had seen in the village school, with shepherds leading their flocks across bright green hills lush as an English meadow in spring.

Frances's isolation from the world was, however, invaded one autumn day in 1918 by the arrival at the farm of a visitor in khaki, puttees and an army knapsack. This was Samuel, a former farmworker who had left West Chapple when she was not yet seven, and who had now returned from the Great War. She had associated the war with the images evoked by rousing hymns at evensong and the vicar's exhortations to remember the sons of England on the battlefields and the high seas. Frances was startled at the leanness of the soldier and the wild and exhausted look in his eye like a hungry buzzard. His skin was tanned to a dark mahogany and there were weather-beaten lines around his mouth and eyes. Sitting at the old deal kitchen table he told Wilmot and Frances about the heat of the desert in Palestine, and about the rats and the shell-holes in France. He talked of the bodies of young men stacked in such great mounds one upon another that it 'made one wonder if there could be a God'.

When Robert John came in for his dinner Samuel was still there at the table, his kit spread about him and no food prepared. The young man leapt to his feet, straightening his shoulders. Robert John greeted him solemnly but in an instant expressed disapproval. Why was there no dinner on the table? Had Frances nothing better to do than sit sprawled at the empty table?

The two men went out into the yard and there was a harsh conversation between them. No, there was no work on the farm, Robert John told him emphatically. Samuel did not give in easily: he would work just for his food and somewhere to lay his head. Surely there was work in many parts of the farm: hedges to be laid or carpentry and building jobs? He was willing and capable of anything. But Robert John was adamant, and at last the soldier's boots could be heard retreating across the cobbled yard.

That night Frances turned over in her mind the visions of war and foreign lands. She was filled with a deep sadness about the returned soldier. Where did he lay his head that night? Had he a family and a home? Was he sleeping under the stars or marching across the county in the dark. She wrote of Samuel's visit in her commonplace book.

The soldier's visit was the first of many such from young men home from the war. As the months went by, figures would appear at the kitchen window, invariably in ragged civilian clothes. The man would hang about uncertainly, offer all manner of services, be given a cup of water and a hunk of dry bread to be eaten in the barn across the yard with the other labourers and the dogs, and then be sent on his way.

Most of the children at the village school lived in Winkleigh itself and could be in the school playground within minutes of leaving their front doors. Frances had to walk two miles, often in snow or drenching rain, and at times in darkness. To reach school by 8.30 in the morning she left the house at seven o'clock before the family had eaten breakfast. She crossed the yard and entered the winding lane to the still, dark pool with its overhanging beech trees and ivy creeping like serpents round the trunks. Upon the next rise was Lute House, the ancient homestead of the Luxtons but now too small for a respectable yeoman's family house.

The lane was now flanked by steep banks topped with hedges, bordering the steep meadows where the Luxtons grazed their old Ruby Reds: there was shade in plenty at the bottom of these fields – ancient oaks, sycamore and ash – and

a stream that gushed along the margin, providing water even
in the height of the parched summer.

At length the lane dipped until it met the stream and here
she had to cross by a pair of stepping-stones and follow the
hedge bordering a neighbour's field until she came to yet
another lane, not a thoroughfare but an ancient cattle-way
between meadows.

At last she came out on to the Winkleigh road and could see
the village with its crazy roof-tops and lofty elms huddling
below the church tower and the chimney-pots streaming
smoke in the wind.

It is clear from Frances's school reports that she was quick
and alert and had a good start on the others of her age, her
mother having taught her to read early. There were two
classes in the school, one taking children from seven to ten, the
other from ten to fourteen. Frances spent some of her time
teaching others to read from ancient primers with large bold
letters. Her contemporaries remember her as a little proud and
aloof, a 'typical Luxton'. At lunchtime most of the children
went home to their mothers, for there were no school meals.
Frances took her satchel with a packed lunch to the Lanes (the
bachelor brother and spinster sister who were to meet with a
tragic end). She sat in the kitchen with Mrs Richards, the
cook, and ate her bread and cheese.

Three years after she started school Robbie joined her on
the journey to Winkleigh and in the classroom. At school they
sat together during his first year, studying from the same book
and the same slate, and they ate their lunch together at the
Lanes'. Robbie's devotion to his sister became proverbial.

Frances had a number of stories about their childhood. She
told the following to several of her acquaintances. It was
the week following haymaking, and both Robert John and
Wilmot had fallen heavily asleep in their armchairs in the
parlour after Sunday lunch. Robbie lay curled up at their feet,

also fast asleep. Frances felt restless and left the house to go for a walk. She wandered across the fields and entered Chapple Wood. She had been walking for some time in the depths of the wood when she was startled by a ragged man with a shaggy beard and wild staring eyes. He was very still, as if paralysed, and he held in one hand a rabbit with its entrails half out and in the other a knife covered in blood. He was one of the many tramps who wandered the West Country in those days, living rough and occasionally begging at the doors of religious houses.

Frances at first recoiled from him in horror at his appearance, but she was not frightened of him. They struck up a conversation and he took her to see his encampment which he had built with cardboard, sacking and leaves. He showed her how he built his fire and, squatting on his haunches, told her about his wandering life and asked her a lot of questions about West Chapple. She stayed with him a long time and when she got up to go he called after her to come and see him again.

When she got back to the house she expected her mother to be angry with her – to ask where she had been. But Wilmot simply said, 'Where's Robbie, then? We thought he was with you?'

They called for him in the apple-room and the barns, they searched in the orchard. Thinking that Robbie had gone in search of her, Frances decided to follow the path to Winkleigh, for it was the one route beyond the farmyard that Robbie knew. She ran all the way to Winkleigh, called at the Lanes', searched the school-yards, the church and the graveyard, but he was nowhere to be found.

On her way back she came upon her parents calling out in the fields. They turned back together when they heard that Frances had been all the way to Winkleigh.

When they reached the yard Frances saw that Robbie was there with a strange man. He was a farmer from Dolton way

who had found Robbie in one of his meadows, weeping and
calling out by a sheep-well. Searching for Frances he had
wandered into the deep fold of a great field. Terrified and lost,
he had just sat calling out until the farmer came by. Frances
remembered that despite their relief her parents suddenly
grew embarrassed at the presence of the stranger, who was
neither invited in nor taken by the hand.

Only later did Frances hear that in the search for Robbie
their father had stumbled on the vagabond, who had been sent
packing. In the weeks that followed Frances returned there
frequently and left food in a biscuit tin, but it was always left
untouched.

Alan Luxton was born when Frances was thirteen. He was a
late child: Robert John was now almost fifty and Wilmot was
forty years of age. After Alan's birth Wilmot became visibly
aged and beset with ailments.

Frances brought up Alan, who was always known simply as
'Baby', and was a mother to him, washing and dressing him
in the morning, feeding him and taking him for walks in the
garden. Robert John, too, relied heavily upon her: she
prepared his meals and washed his clothes and bore the brunt,
increasingly, of his moods. And the more she acted as a
surrogate mother for Alan and a substitute wife for Robert
John, the more possessive and jealous Robert John became
towards her. Yet it was rarely with the possessiveness of loving
kindness. Frances told Irene Brown that when she was twenty-
one he said: 'Nobody will have you for a wife. You're very dear
to me, but you're not the most beautiful of creatures. Anyway
you don't want to get married. You've got everything you
need here. You'll always have your brothers and the house.'

In the early years of the twenties Frances had little chance
of meeting a husband, preoccupied as she was with household
duties. For a brief period Robbie departed to a boarding

school at West Buckland and she missed him keenly, writing affectionate letters to him weekly, but he was not to remain away for long. After two years Robert John evidently lost his nerve and notified the headmaster that he was taking the boy away. It was a decision that provoked an agitated letter from the headmaster. The letter, along with Robbie's school reports, survived among the family papers. It is dated 2 December 1926:

Dear Mr Luxton,

I thought I would write an [*sic*] suggest to you that you give you [*sic*] boy a longer period at school. He is not yet 16 and it does seem a pity not to give a boy a chance of a really good education to day [*sic*], without which he can go a very little way. Supposing for instance he becomes a farmer, I think you will admit that at the present time the farmer having much more public work to perform than before, must be a man of education. He is getting on quite well in school and has developed in very good lines and if you could leave him until seventeen, you would have no cause to regret the result. I have had now a great many years experience in teaching and I doubt very much if any boy has much chance of doing very well today if he leaves school before that age.

Apart from the question of in school work, I hold very strongly the opinion that a boy should never leave school until he is on the verge of manhood and so has learnt to avoid the numerous pitfalls of life, which cause a great deal of trouble in this land among youths. Hoping that you will give this letter your consideration.

Yours sincerely,

Ernest C. Harries

Robbie was not allowed to stay on. He came home to work side by side with his father in the fields and learn farming. Robert John's instructions were deeply rooted in traditional ways and admitted little experiment. There were hundreds of pages of notes written out in the farm diaries which went back to the eighteenth century. Here are some transcriptions from a notebook dated 1825 and still in use at West Chapple in the mid seventies.

Lime and lime without manure will make both farm and farmer poor.

To destroy the worms or batts in horses cut a handful of the tops of Box chop it small mix it with the corn and a quantity of urine give it them every other morning for some days and you may depend upon a cure. Tried the same myself and have always succeeded – you may give some of the best flour of Brimstone in their Corn at times.

To destroy Foxes
Take 3 or 4 fresh Moles, take a quill and put some poison in it, put the one end of the quill into the fundament of the Mole and blow the poison into its inside, throw the Moles where you conceive the Foxes come and it is certain death.

A Recipe to decoy Hares
One Ounce of the Oil of Parsley
20 drops of the Oil of Rhodium
20 drops of the Oil of Thyme
10 drops of the Oil of Annis
mix them together in the same bottle then take a bunch of parsley, tie it with a string and drop a few drops of the above Oils on the parsley, and likewise strike your shoes and hands drag the parsley along the ground round any woods, or places where you think any hares, or rabbits, resort, into any convenient wheat or clover field, so that they may have feed, then have netts and lay them at the gateways etc, and drive the field you will easily take them; or strike the wires with the oils, and you will be certain. Be sure to strike your hands and shoes with oils.

To draw Moles into snaps
One ounce of the Oil of Earth worm
twenty drops of the Oil of Annis
ten drops of the Oil of Musk

Mix them together and strike the tiller of the snap which you will find a certain enticement.

A certain cure for the Cholic in a Horse. Take one quart of strong beer, two glasses of distilled liquor or strong gin, half an ounce of the Oil of Carraway, or the Oil of Annis seed, boil them together, let it be cool enough and drench your horse with it, in about an hour afterwards give him a warm mash of oats and bran; but previous to the drench, take three quarts of blood from him. Be sure not to give him cold water for a day or two.

As he got older Robbie grew increasingly attached to Frances and dependent on her emotionally. A cousin who used to visit regularly during this period remembers the way he would sit and gaze at her, smiling affectionately, and how they exchanged loving, 'knowing' looks. 'I thought even then that there was more than a mere brotherly and sisterly affection.'

Neither then, as Robbie progressed into adolescence, nor later in life did he express any interest in women, nor indeed friendship outside the family. Years later when he got engaged, Alan told one of his Knapman cousins that Robert John had said: 'There is no need to gratify sexual appetite with a woman. Marriage is expensive and a nuisance – there are other ways of overcoming the needs of the flesh.'

Frances, on the other hand, longed to meet new people, longed to travel, and daydreamed endlessly about marriage. She told Irene Brown that when she was twenty a cousin from Coldridge called on them one Sunday afternoon in best suit and shiny shoes. It was clear that he had been sent over to spy out the land and make appraisal of Frances. Instead of welcoming the young man, Robert John interrogated him aggressively. The youth was too shy and respectful of his uncle even to reply; he retreated, crimson and tongue-tied, after an hour.

Another cousin who appeared at regular intervals during these years was William Luxton. His first visit was one summer's afternoon in 1929. The sheer novelty of having a young man from London put the household in a spin. William remembers that Robert John was 'all smiles' for the first half-hour as he spoke of the old times and revived memories of William's father. He was the 'epitome of the indulgent uncle' with his bright red face and white walrus moustache, and Wilmot spread a generous tea with home-made bread, scones, jam and cakes and Devon cream.

But when William started to talk of his life in London, of evenings at the theatre and music halls, Robert's affability turned to scowling thunder. The boys disappeared and Frances looked at first worried then depressed. Robert John was restless, stamping from the parlour to the kitchen muttering oaths and execrations at Wilmot and Frances. Several times William heard dishes being broken and the strange sound of Robert John hissing through his teeth. Nevertheless William Luxton stayed the night, sleeping in the tiny box-room, a rare occurrence indeed at West Chapple. He got to know Frances and the boys on their own as he went walking with them down the lane to Chub House between tea and bedtime. He was astonished at their rusticity and innocence. He thought Frances had natural wit and charm, and that she seemed ready 'to break out'.

The economic depression of the thirties only exacerbated Robert John's tendency to distrust outsiders and to become ever more entrenched in his own way of doing things. He steadfastly refused to have mains water and electricity in-stalled; he refused to communicate with the outside world (except for the sale of farm produce) and would not answer government or council inquiries. Robbie told Fred Lyne that a union representative one day approached Robert John in the yard thinking he was a farm labourer. He asked him with a conspiratorial wink whether he was unionized. Without a

word Robert John walked into the house and reappeared with
a shotgun.

Throughout the inter-war period Robbie worked the land
with his father and Alan went to the village school in Winkleigh. Frances, meanwhile, was growing impatient with her
father and bitter about her prospects. Without seeking his
approval she joined the Devon County Dairy School at
Crediton, as much to meet new faces as to learn about modern
dairy practice. Mrs Molland of Winkleigh joined the school
at the same time and remembers Frances well. At about this
time Frances became interested in riding. The Luxtons had a
mild old brood mare called Tidy that occasionally pulled the
trap. Frances salvaged some ancient tack and taught herself
to ride. Out on the horse one day she met Henry Chambers,
a local boy who worked on a neighbouring farm. Soon the
story of their 'romance' was all over Winkleigh. Then Robert
John took a resourceful measure to thwart her. He too would
go riding. To this day Winkleigh people remember Robert
John hacking along behind her, cursing and groaning as he
went. They also remember Frances walking with Henry down
the lane towards Winkleigh with Robert John following
behind on horseback. The 'romance' did not survive.

One of the results of joining the Dairy School was that
Frances made a friend in Edith Saunders. They saw each other
rarely as Edith lived at Crediton, but they corresponded
regularly. It was through Edith that Frances escaped from
home for the first time in her life. Edith belonged to the
Cooperative Holiday Association, which organized vacations
for young women in various parts of the British Isles and
Europe. The advantage of the system was that one could pay
for the holiday on the 'never-never'. It took Frances three years
– from 1935 to 1938 – to save for an eight-day holiday in
Scotland, and even then Robert John only consented because
he felt too ill and wretched to summon the energy to object.

Armed with a box camera, a travelling rug and a cardboard suitcase, with one pound in her pocket, Frances set off on the first holiday of her life. She had never been to Exeter, let alone London or Scotland. Promising her mother that she would write every day, she set off on foot for Winkleigh and thence by bus to Eggesford to catch a train for Exeter, and then on to London. She travelled up to Edinburgh with Edith and then by bus to Ardenconnel at Rhu in Dunbartonshire, where they stayed in a large bleak country house, a cross between a youth hostel and a convent school for girls.

It rained long and heavily in the intervals between violent thunderstorms. Frances and Edith visited Glasgow – 'there is hardly a break in the houses between here and the city' – where they wandered around Woolworth's and the Cathedral.

Frances wrote home to the family every day: 'We are about 630 miles from Winkleigh. I slept well on the train on Friday night, the rug was very useful. There is a lot of hay and corn about here also saw a good deal coming up in the train to London. Here they make the hay into large stooks and tie them across and around with ropes and chains.'

In her first letter she signed off with a plea for cash: 'When you write Dad can put in a £1 note if he likes. I've had to get a thing or two but I don't think it is necessary to register it nobody will know if it is there.'

Four days later she wrote again: 'Very many thanks for empty envelope received this morning, it looks to me that you forgot to put the letter in, it does not appear to have been sealed.' She complained that Edith, who shared a room with her, snored badly and that she had to wake her during the night. She also noted that many of the girls sent off 'as many as twenty postcards at a time, and they write and receive heaps of letters'. She was awed by the three-course meals and the availability of unlimited hot baths. It was the first proper bath she had had in her life.

1 *Lawrence Luxton, grandfather*

2 *Robert John Luxton, his two sisters Fanny and Pollie (Mary Louisa)
and an unidentified boy, probably a cousin, at West Chapple, c. 1900*

3 *The Luxtons, 1914: Robert John holding Robbie; Frances and Wilmot*

4 *Winkleigh Square, c. 1910*

5 *Winkleigh Square, c. 1910*

6 above *Winkleigh Church gate, c. 1910*

7 left *'Baby Alan' and Wilmot, 1925*

8 right *Frances and Robbie Luxton aged seven and four*

9 left *Alan Luxton, aged four,*
in the yard where he died fifty years later

10 above *Alan, 1928*

11 above *Alan and Frances*, c. *1928*

12 right *Frances Luxton with her mother Wilmot*, c. *1930*

13 left *Robbie Luxton,*
c. *1934*

14 below *Alan* (right) *with
members of the Young
Farmers Club, 1946*

15 right *Brushford Barton*

16 below right
West Chapple Farm,
c. *1930*

17 *West Chapple in 1977 shortly after John Gledhill bought the farm*

18 *Lute House at West Chapple Farm*

19 *The old thresher and crusher in working order
at the time of the Luxtons' deaths*

20 *left* *The water-wheel which provided energy for the farm. John Gledhill wired off the entrance*

21 *right* *Detective Chief Superintendent Proven Sharpe*

22 *below* *Scene from Bob Bentley's* The Recluse *(Twentieth Century-Fox, 1981) filmed on location at West Chapple Farm*

23 *overleaf* *A lane near Winkleigh*

Every day it rained with a driving wind. Day after day their
outings and picnics were cancelled; but they braved the Kyles
of Bute and Loch Fyne, and walked in the teeth of a gale about
the hills of Rhu. In the evening there were sing-songs and
whist drives, and prayers. Frances had turned into a pretty
and resourceful young woman and the holiday was not without its adventures. Among a small collection of misty snaps
taken through sheets of rain there is one of Frances and Edith
with two young men, sitting huddled together on a coil of rope
aboard a Loch steamer.

According to Edith, Frances returned the following Saturday to a glum reception at West Chapple. Robert John had
had a slight stroke and was propped up in bed defiant and
refusing to see a doctor; his face sagged and he was full of
bitterness at Frances's selfishness and betrayal.

Frances was now tending two self-centred invalids as well
as looking after the boys, who had taken over the running of
the farm.

The winter passed in misery. Robert John called out con-
tinually for attention and detained Frances at his bedside with
interminable harangues about the farm, the land and his
inheritance. He constantly fiddled with family papers,
rearranging them and scribbling indecipherable hieroglyphics
in the margins. He was for ever fidgeting with his will, reading
it aloud and fretting over its provisions. He seemed obsessed
with the idea of preserving the integrity of West Chapple, of
not losing one inch of land.

Wilmot, too, had taken to her bed in the parlour, but her
troubles appeared more mental than physical. She harped on
the days of her teens when she was beautiful and properly
'finished', one of Miss Powlerland's favourites.

Robbie was now following the pattern set by his father: up
at six o'clock and out in the yard and the fields. He was twenty-
seven years of age, tough, energetic and ill-tempered – and by
evening haggard with hard work. He was totally reliant on

Frances for his domestic comforts, and for his emotional
comforts too.

Alan, now in his seventeenth year, was mostly silent and
morose, working under his brother's command. Sam Lendon
and other neighbours say that Frances fussed him and tried to
give him a lot of her time, which he took with a poor grace;
while Robbie, who was jealous of any attention Frances gave
to others, treated Alan as a child – albeit a child who could do
a full day's work. Robbie could always put Alan into a rage
and send him storming into the house by calling him 'Baby',
the family's name for him throughout his childhood.

Robert John died of pneumonia on 2 May 1939. Wilmot
rallied to put on a face for the funeral. She invited some of her
relations and friends and they came back to West Chapple
after the funeral for tea. She sat like a comic tragedy queen in
a long old-fashioned dress and black straw hat decorated with
paper violets. It was the last any of those guests would see of
the house. The effort broke something inside Wilmot. She
retreated into an irreversible depression and never left her bed
again.

Despite the outbreak of war Robbie was determined that
life would go on as usual. The land had to be farmed as it
always had been. But this war was different, and threatened
to touch everybody in the British Isles, even in remote Devon.
In the spring of 1940 a family of Cockneys called Taylor was
settled at Lute House by the billeting officer. It was a large
family of eight children and the house had only two bedrooms;
the paths of the Luxtons and of the Taylors were bound to
cross. The situation did not suit Robbie, for it meant a constant
trail of strangers through his farmyard, and the threat of gates
left open and apples scrumped from the orchard. The arrangement was far more ominous for Alan, however, as Lute House
had been left to him by his father along with virtually half of

all Chapple land, although, according to the will, none of this property could be sold without Robbie's permission.

To a farming family which had schooled itself in self-sufficiency and survival over fifty years, had passed through the depression of the thirties and hardly noticed it, the economies imposed on wartime Britain were scarcely harsh. In fact, things looked up on the cash side as black marketeers found their way to West Chapple farmyard looking for bacon and eggs. The Luxtons, who never enjoyed such luxuries themselves, were delighted to find that the asking price soared ever higher.

More profound changes were to come later in the war, however. In September 1942 teams of workers were encamped on the heath north of West Chapple; they had brought bull-dozers, tar-making machines and building materials. Border-ing the Luxtons' land and virtually in sight of the West Chapple farmhouse, engineers of the United States Air Force laid out an airfield with runways, anti-aircraft installations, firing ranges, bunkers, searchlights and Nissen huts. Across the Luxton fields wafted the sound of Glen Miller's jazz; and then in 1943 came the roar of aircraft, flying in and taking off all day and all night as the Americans prepared for D-Day. Alan was now in his early twenties, young enough to begin to think that this was the normal world. He mixed with airmen at the King's Arms and the Winkleigh Hotel. He smoked Camels and Lucky Strikes and bartered best bacon, fresh eggs and clotted cream for American ties and T-shirts. He learnt about the great wheat plains of the Mid-West from men who had sat aloft combine harvesters. His imagination ranged over the awesome possibilities of proper, modern farming after the war.

Then, suddenly, the Americans had gone and in their place in February 1944 came the Royal Canadian Air Force Lynx Squadron flying night and day sorties to the Brest peninsula. Now it was Frances's turn to be affected. She had spent the war working on the farm like any man, sometimes from six in the morning until midnight. In addition she had to find time to cook, clean the house and care for old Wilmot who lay upstairs. But some time in 1944 she met a Canadian airman called Mike McCallum from Montreal. It is impossible to say how often and where they met, or whether they were lovers, but after the war he continued to write postcards to her until 1965 when they stopped abruptly.

With the end of the war the airfield was closed down: the runways became overgrown; most of the Nissen huts were removed; a few were turned into chicken houses. The heath returned to its centuries-long neglect. The evacuees returned to the 'Smoke', and Lute House, considerably the worse for wear, was abandoned to the damp, the rats and the ravages of dry rot.

Wilmot was eventually to die of cancer of the uterus. She was buried with scant ceremony among snowdrifts in Winkleigh churchyard, and Robbie – who up to now had continued to share a bed with Alan – moved into his mother's room and slept in the 'Maister's' bed at last.

Victory Day was celebrated in Winkleigh with a grand fête, a children's tea party and fancy-dress parade. In the evening there was a bonfire and dancing. Robbie worked on at West Chapple as usual. Frances and Alan helped with the children's celebrations and danced and drank till after midnight with the rest of the village. Every farmer for miles around had brought several flagons of heady cider and there would be splitting headaches in the morning.

For Frances and Alan the celebration might have marked the beginning of a new era. Life had been hard and uncertain for everybody during the war, but many of the social barriers had been broken down and there was a new sense of camaraderie flourishing even in rural communities like Winkleigh. Large numbers of men who had worked the land before the war would soon be back from overseas; they would surely not return to the semi-slavery of pre-war labouring; nor would daughters who had lived away from home as land-girls and munitions workers be content with the farmhouse kitchen and the apron. The advent of full-blown socialism seemed a certainty, and with it, or so it seemed in the summer of 1945, would come nationalization of farmland and farming.

Robbie had always regarded the government as just another outsider. What had the government ever done for him? As for nationalization, he had been born into a family steeped in the tradition of ownership and inheritance. For generations the Luxtons had identified themselves completely with the soil, their own soil; it was unthinkable that a government should come and take away the soil that he and his forebears had sweated for over the centuries. The end of the war saw Robbie reverting to the model of life established by his father. He made a number of changes in the routine of the farm and the household that emphasized a return to the old pattern. He had the sign taken down from the gate leading into the farm. Then he had a great old five-barred gate erected by the side of Chub House. Robbie explained that the rough ground alongside the lane leading from Chub to Chapple would provide excellent grass and he wanted to turn sheep out there at regular intervals. He wanted no tourists or outsiders wandering through, and the inner gate must be shut at all times. It was this device that made any visitor or 'wanderer' think that the entrance to West Chapple was the entrance to a quiet meadow. One certainly would never have thought of taking a car through that gate.

Alan, who was now twenty-four, was being paid ten shillings a week for a work-load that was seldom less than twelve hours a day, six days a week, and even on Sundays he was expected to help out with feeding the animals. The farm still lacked a tractor, relying instead on draught horses. There was no mains water or electricity. The two farm labourers –

one living in Winkleigh, the other at Chub House – slaved alongside Robbie and Alan, and sometimes Frances. The clearing of waste land, wood-cutting, hedging and ditching took up much of the winter; much of the haymaking was still done by hand.

Robbie argued that he was giving Alan a roof over his head, keeping him in food, providing him – through the services of Frances – with laundry and cleaning and cooking. Robbie even bought Alan his clothes, deducting their value from his wages. The items were carefully recorded in the farm ledgers.

Alan, who had been classed as an essential worker in 1940, had not complained about his lot during the war years. He had been bitterly disappointed at missing the opportunity of going overseas, but he felt that living at home in safety he had much to be thankful for. After the war, however, he took a different view of things, and then the rows started.

Alan joined the Young Farmers' Club in Winkleigh; he started reading the newspapers and taking an active part in Labour Party politics, although by this stage it was clear that the new government was *not* going to nationalize land after all. He learnt with excitement about the new grants available for farm improvements and began to map out plans and improvements for West Chapple Farm – perhaps the first time in a hundred years that this had been done. Some of his ideas are listed in his neat hand on a loose leaf in one of the farm notebooks:

   Alteration and reconditioning of Lute House
   Making of Bridge over stream in lane
   Improving farm road
   Making culvert over stream in lane
   Removal of three hedges
   Removal of stumps
   Pest destruction
   Clearing of waste land.

The items were listed under Ministry reference number H 25, which referred to the government's grant scheme for agricultural improvements.

Lute House was, in fact, in an appalling state of dereliction. It belonged to Alan by right, and he wanted to renovate it and live there. He envisaged doing his own chores, keeping his own poultry and having a measure of independence. But Robbie was utterly opposed to the idea. Lute House, in his view, would make an excellent barn or storehouse; it might not be suitable for human habitation, but it would probably stand for ever as a barn. Why spend hard-earned cash on renovation and rates? Whatever was spent would have to come out of the farm.

There were scenes of fury at mealtimes, terrible rows that went on far into the night, but Robbie would not be budged. His word, in any case, was final because he controlled the purse-strings except for a small income from rent in Winkleigh that Frances had inherited from her mother.

The country was now in the grip of the Labour Government's post-war austerity programme, with shortages of every sort of consumer durable, including clothes, furniture and domestic utensils and appliances. What was the sense of setting up home in such times as these? asked Robbie. Nothing should be spent; everyone must expect life to be full of sacrifices. And here was Alan demanding high wages and large sums to be spent on a separate establishment. Next thing he'd want a clothes allowance and trips abroad.

Some of Alan's friends from the Winkleigh Young Farmers days vividly remember Alan and the stories he told of his battles with Robbie. They say that during the late forties Alan was an energetic, open-hearted young man who loved to mix socially and who had ambitions. Even the harsh régime of work at West Chapple failed to quench his appetite for friends and a full social life. He might have risen at six in the morning, fed and watered cattle until dawn and then worked in the

freezing mud cleaning out a ditch all day, but in the evening
he would scrub himself down and be off to Winkleigh in
all weathers on his ancient bicycle to attend a parish social
or meet his friends in the King's Arms. He drank strong
cider and, like many farmworkers, he smoked fiendishly and
gave away as many as he smoked himself. He easily got
through the wages that Robbie paid him by the middle of
the week, and Frances helped him secretively with her own
money.

The older and stronger Alan grew, and the more he mixed
in the outside world, the less prepared he was to endure
Robbie's attempts to run his life. Visitors to the farm in those
days remember rows between the brothers – in the yard and
even in public down at the sheep dip. Often the source of
dissension was how they should do things, with Alan urging
that they should invest in mechanization, fertilizers, insecti-
cides and new breeds of cattle.

Things improved for a time, it is remembered, when
Frances bought Alan an old 1920s Austin. It was a great black
hearse of a motoring car with broken seats and a clapped-out
engine that belched smoke and guzzled oil; but Alan was in
heaven. From the day the 'old Bus' arrived Alan was scarcely
to be seen. Either his head was hidden under the bonnet (a
necessary preliminary to any journey) or he was bowling down
the narrow lanes to Winkleigh and far beyond – to Okehampton, Crediton and Exeter.

Frances was now in her early forties and still a fine-looking
woman with hair that shone like burnished copper. She had
no social life except for church on Sundays. She was still robust
and attractive and longed to have children, but she must have
seen life slipping by as she sacrificed herself for her brothers.
After the old car arrived Alan was probably more able to
endure Robbie's thunder, but it is likely that she now came in
for the full brunt of it.

She did most of the cleaning, the washing and the cooking. She was always on hand to work on the farm, especially during the lambing season when she would be out at four o'clock in the morning taking over from Alan or Robbie who had been up all night. She spent many hours in all weathers in the vegetable garden digging and hoing the soil, growing cabbages and turnips and potatoes. It was perhaps in revolt against this constant grind that she left the brothers and set off for her cousins in Highbury, where she made the acquaintance of Captain Wagemaker.

William Luxton remembers the Captain and recollects Frances's visit. Wagemaker was a tough old sailor, but he had a courtly manner and knew how to pass a compliment. He was magnificently dressed in tailored shirts and expensive well-cut suits. His cravat was always fixed with a diamond tie-pin, and he played with an enormous gold pocket watch. According to William Luxton, he was on the look-out for a new wife – although failing that a competent housekeeper would have done just as well. It must have been an entirely novel experience for Frances to meet a man who made her feel ladylike, attractive and interesting. Wagemaker, the much-travelled, opinionated old sea captain, was a gifted raconteur, and here was an eager listener to whom he could tell his best stories afresh. Frances stayed on in Highbury for the rest of the week and by the time she left he had taken her on a verbal tour of the world. The interests and conversations of the men Frances lived with seldom penetrated beyond Chub House, so Wagemaker must have struck her as a very romantic character. They promised to write and to meet again, and it is clear from Wagemaker's correspondence that the possibility of marriage hovered gently at the back of their minds. Over the next six years her correspondence with him would be her only contact with the world beyond Winkleigh. She wrote to him at least once a week and letters and postcards arrived at

West Chapple with exotic stamps from every corner of the globe.

The trip to London, and the initiation of the Captain's correspondence, may well have brought home to Robbie, as no amount of complaining on her part could have done, that he could no longer take Frances's presence and services for granted. To lose Frances would be unthinkable: it was not just her usefulness in the house and on the farm; the truth was he loved her deeply and needed her. He had no desire for a wife. Frances was everything to him. In the early fifties Robbie became more gentle and affectionate towards his sister. All who met them in subsequent years remarked on the strong and loving bond that existed between them at all times.

Life at West Chapple Farm improved and even became fairly contented until one afternoon in the spring of 1953 when Alan asked Frances if she would lend him the money to buy an engagement ring. Frances did more than that, she went with him to Exeter and helped choose it.

Alan's fiancée was Myrtle Standbury, a Winkleigh girl who mixed with the Young Farmers' Club crowd. To those who knew them it seemed a suitable match in every way, and they were both apparently very much in love. But the implications of the marriage were ominous indeed for West Chapple Farm. The interview between the two brothers, when it came, must have gone very badly. According to all who know the story of the engagement, Alan's request was straightforward. He wanted to sell his share in the farm to Robbie and Frances and make a completely new life for himself and Myrtle.

But Robbie, it seemed, immediately ruled out any possibility of buying Alan's share. In the mid fifties Robbie Luxton had about £200 in cash, which was kept in a safe in the house, and about £800 in the form of securities and bonds. Alan had estimated his share of the farm, including stock, as worth

£6,000. Robbie and Frances would have been obliged to borrow the money to buy Alan out, and this Robbie absolutely refused to do. It would have been kinder, perhaps, had Robert John left the entire property to Robbie from the start. As it was, the portion left to Alan, with restricting clauses, could serve only to tantalize and torture him throughout his life.

Instead Robbie apparently made a counter-proposal – that Alan should, as he had earlier suggested, move into Lute House. They would work together and renovate the house, then they would continue as partners. One day Alan would inherit the whole farm; according to Robbie he owed it to his ancestors and his children to help maintain Chapple and to pass it on intact, as their father had done, and his father before him.

Alan clearly had no intention of continuing the unequal partnership with his brother. Their views on farming were too opposed, and Robbie's attitude towards money was likely to be just as unrelenting after Alan had married. No, it was too late to start talking about Lute House. The fair, the honourable thing was to set him free. Alan, it seemed, had it all planned. He would borrow more money, and with this and the money from his portion of West Chapple would purchase a smaller grassland farm of 150 acres. He would buy a cheap property that needed turning round, and he would use every modern aid and government grant available. He would not miss a trick. Fred Lyne, who came to the farm in 1950, remembers that the argument continued to and fro for weeks; it usually started at mealtimes and continued out into the yard and the fields. Frances refused to take sides when all three were together, but she sided with Alan when she spoke to Robbie alone.

It must have been clear all along that Robbie would never give way. He was not a vindictive or vicious man, but he loved West Chapple with an almost religious passion and conviction.

It seems that it was not simply that he did not believe in borrowing money, but that the idea of borrowing on the security of West Chapple was sacrilegious. It was putting the land of his forefathers at risk; it was surrendering control to the fly-by-night moneylenders who would like nothing better than to see him fail on his repayments. Robbie had been brought up at his father's knee on stories such as this. Did Alan really know what he was asking? How could he possibly put West Chapple at such a risk even if it was to marry the girl he loved?

According to several accounts they came to blows in the end. Returning home one night full of cider, Alan staggered into Robbie's bedroom and demanded his share of his father's inheritance there and then; neither of them would leave the room, he said, until Robbie gave in. Robbie leapt out of bed and their struggle developed into a fist fight in the dark. Both were hardened and strong with years of labour outdoors; one of them might have killed the other had not Frances managed to come between them. Then the arguments ended; Alan saw that it was hopeless.

For several weeks Alan seethed in silent rage. Then he came home one day with the ring in his pocket. Frances kept it in a drawer in her bedroom until the day she died. According to Fred Lyne, Alan now refused to eat as well as speak and ceased working on the farm. Most days he stayed in bed. Sometimes he could be heard from the yard yelling at his brother. Frances told Lyne once that Alan would not allow her into the room to change his clothes or even to bring him tea. Sometimes he burnt the sheets with his cigarettes.

He had gone down to about eight stone and was filthy and stinking when Frances finally brought the doctor to him. A severe mental illness was diagnosed and he was eventually persuaded to take treatment as a private patient in an asylum in Exeter. According to several accounts he had electric shock therapy. Lyne remembers that when Alan returned to the farm his clothes hung on him like old sacking and his boot-laces were permanently undone. He seemed stooped and round-shouldered.

Alan apparently did not speak for several weeks. Then for several weeks more he did not stop speaking. The Luxtons' cousin, Fred Knapman, says that he seemed obsessed with the idea that women were evil, that everything was the fault of women. He now started to fill his day making notes in a spring-back binder with the title *The Truth about Women*. He ransacked the Bible searching for quotations that supported his misogyny.

Frances and Robbie soon discovered that Alan was unlikely to return to his old self. He talked to himself a great deal and kept to his room for days on end. Then he would suddenly appear normal and show an interest in the farm. 'What needs doing, then?' he would ask Fred Lyne with a sheepish look. He could continue in this normal state for days on end, unless a visitor turned up unexpectedly in the yard. Then he would hide, either in his room or in one of the sheds, or if he were caught out in the open he would shout abuse, not necessarily at the visitor but at the trees and roof-tops. Alan became an additional reason for discouraging the outside world from visiting the farm.

In his lucid, normal phases Alan could even hold a conversation in a halting sort of way. He liked to ask questions about the farm and the animals, and, while he would never contribute an opinion, he would repeat back what had been said to him if he agreed with it. At times, working out in the yard or in the fields, he would lose his temper violently if he thought things were not being done the right way. Then he would shout at Robbie and call him an old fool, or storm back to the house and lock himself in his room.

Alan could not be relied upon to work consistently by himself any distance from the yard. He would offer to do jobs, insist aggressively upon doing them, but Robbie and Fred Lyne would come upon the job only half done some days later. Alan had lost his old stamina and strength and consistency. His illness meant that everybody else had to work much harder; it meant that at times Alan would hold them up from completing a job swiftly and efficiently; but Robbie bore the new situation with resignation.

When Frances brought Alan home and installed him again in his bedroom she must have known that the course of her own life was now set until the day she died. Alan was as well as he would ever be, and even if he got no worse he would require constant care and affection.

Fred Lyne

One afternoon towards the end of my research I visited West Chapple to walk the farm and gather some final impressions. It was now late October, but the sun still shone warmly and there were hosts of midges rising and falling in the woods. In the deserted fields clumps of decaying thistles and dark seeded nettles rose above the lush grass and clover. Occasionally a cock pheasant would rise complaining from the hedgerows and the crows groused and circled above the woods. I had walked the outer fields and been astonished at the number of small 'garden' gates erected for short cuts by the Luxtons; frequently I had paused on the summits of the steep fields to look out towards Dartmoor, melancholy in the hazy autumn light. Arriving back in the yard outside the farmhouse I was surprised to find Fred Lyne seated by the sheep-well. He was sorting through a collection of old tools and I understood at once that he had returned to claim a few items of his own property. He had been quenching his thirst from an enamel mug that stood at the side of the trough and his grimy cap was pulled well down over his eyes.

Grass and plantains now obscured the cobbles; the orchard was matted with bindweed and nettles. Fred had laid several implements on the ground beside him; others that were broken and rusty beyond repair had been thrown on a pile a little distance away. He wore an expression of sadness and bitterness as he scrutinized an old sickle, rubbing at the blade and pressing his thumbnail into the wormy wooden handle.

He nodded with recognition when he saw me and seemed pleased. I sat down next to him and drank some water from

the metal cup. It was very cold and tasted of peat. We sat for
a while in silence; then he said: 'It's strange sitting here thinking of all the years and the way they loved this place. They've
not been dead more than a few weeks and it has changed
already. Something about this place died with them. All that
work and suffering over the years, and what has come out
of it?

'I came to work here at the end of the war and it was a
beautiful farm then. The brothers were young and healthy
and strong, and Frances was a fine woman and very good to
me. She was full of humour and did everything well. She
baked lovely cakes and bread and there was always a welcome
and a kind word from her when I came up in the morning. On
hot summer days she often brought cider and a cake to me out
here by the well, and we've sat together right here and talked.
And on winter afternoons she's come out at dusk and called
me in for a cup of tea by the kitchen fire, and I've gone in in
my old clothes, into that sparkling clean kitchen and sat by the
fire with her. She treated me like a brother, and she admired
her brothers – they were upright, industrious men in those
days.

'It all started to go bad I suppose after Alan fell ill and had
to go to hospital. Well, he came back and he wasn't the same,
and nor were Robbie and Frances. There was a lot of shouting
went on in the house and in the yard. Things weren't easy in
those days. There was more money around, but it wasn't going
into farmers' pockets and the expense of everything was going
up. Robbie and Danovitz and I had to work all the harder
now that Alan wasn't well. Robbie lived for work then; he
seemed determined that the farm wouldn't get on top of him.
He got really tight-fisted; he'd been tight before, but now
nothing missed his eye. It was like a religion with him now.
He was out in all weathers, all times of the night; he got to look
like a weatherbeaten old tree, that hard and gnarled he

looked. He spoke with a cruel tongue about Alan at times, but he made an effort to deal with him kindly when he came out to work with us and wouldn't hear a word against him from us. Robbie, Danovitz and me did the work of six men.

'I never saw much of Frances from that time on. If she was in the yard and saw me coming up the lane, she'd go in the house and shut the door. Those were bad days. Alan would be up in his room roaring and yelling. Then one day I was out here in the shed eating my lunch when she came out and sat with me. She looked at me a while then turned away and started to cry her eyes out. She put her head down into her apron and wept her heart out. She got up and walked to and fro and didn't seem to know what to do with herself. Then she said how God would punish them for what they had done to Alan. They would be cursed not to have children and there would be nobody to carry on the Luxton line at West Chapple. "And what will become of Alan if anything happens to Robbie and me?" All the time she was speaking she was crying, and there was nothing I could think to say to her.

'In the end she dried her eyes and said that she supposed they had a lot to be grateful for: they had the farm and enough to eat, and they had each other. "Anyway," she said, "I dare say Alan will get on the mend and will be himself again." Even though I didn't believe it I said this was very true, and that she should think of that when she felt miserable. She smiled through her tears and up she got and went back into the kitchen. That evening as I was leaving the yard, she came out and said "God bless you, Fred." She was a very good, tender woman.

'I've no memory for the years. But we went on like that for several seasons. Alan got no worse, but he got no better neither.

'Anyway, one day I cut myself badly while hedging up at the top. I came down to bind it up and went to the kitchen door. It was freezing cold and November. Well, she wasn't there but the door was wide open and I stepped across the threshold. Well, I hadn't been in there for a few years. It was a shocking change for the worse. The cooking range was out cold, something you'd never have found in years gone past. She hadn't swept for weeks I shouldn't think; it was freezing cold and dark and miserable in there; there were a few bits of food on the table, and papers piled high as if she'd been turning out drawers. Well, I hung around for a while and called out, then I went up and washed the cut in the trough. It was getting dark and I went back one more time and looked inside. Then I saw her, just a few feet away from me by the dairy door. She was very still and white as a sheet, and she stood watching me a little while. "I'm sorry Fred," she said. "What do you want?" I showed her the cut and she did it for me with a clean rag by the light of a paraffin lamp. It was all so cold and comfortless I felt worried for her. She seemed to guess my thoughts. "You're surprised at how you find me, Fred," she said. "And you have good reason. We will never have children here at West Chapple. But I've prayed and prayed and I know that I can put it right."

'She told me that she was trying to find close cousins to leave the farm to. But it was difficult: so many relatives had died childless, so many had dispersed to the ends of the earth. "But there must be somebody," she said.

'That's when she got into the habit of trailing to churches and graveyards all over Devon. She was trying to piece together the family. In the end, although that was much later, she started to look for Luxtons all over the world. As the years passed she seemed to be more and more low. I saw her only occasionally and she seemed drooped and heavy in her movements, always sighing. She seemed to have lost all her energy. I never got to see inside the house, and I noticed nobody else went inside either. She stopped growing vegetables and tending the chickens and working in the dairy. She was polite but always distant.

'Well, it must have been around the spring of 1967 I came down into the yard one morning and Robbie said, "She's gone, then." "Gone?" I said. "Oh yes. She's gone travelling. Italy, Greece, Middle East, all over."

'He sounded as though he didn't know whether to laugh or cry. But I thought he seemed proud that she had gone, as if he were boasting. She was gone for two or three weeks, I think, and when she came back the difference was amazing. She looked a lot healthier and happier and outward-going, and seemed to be getting back to her old self again. She smartened the place up and Mrs Danovitz started coming up to do cleaning for her. She got interested in the garden again. We talked a bit about her travelling and it was obvious she'd really enjoyed herself. Something had changed in her and she seemed full of hope again.

'Well, from then on it became a regular thing. The next year she was off to Africa and all over. She came back suntanned and really well-looking. She put on weight, filled out, had her hair done, had new frocks and so on. You wouldn't have thought she was the same woman. We had a talk after she returned and she told me she had been looking up relations. She said: "You see, Fred, we were a great family once; I'd love to leave West Chapple to a Luxton who would take it on and carry on where we leave off." She didn't tell me how successful she had been but she certainly didn't seem downhearted. Now Robbie seemed to take it well when she went off. Mind you, I don't think they ate too well while she was away. But Alan was very badly affected; he neglected himself. Sometimes he wouldn't get up out of bed for days on end and you'd hear him talking to himself as you passed below the window. Then he'd come outside and you've never seen anything like it: just an old sack around his middle, another around his shoulders and a pair of old army boots on his feet. He was filthy, unshaven and foul-mouthed.

'Well, the more she went off the more she changed, it seemed to me. When she came back she went straight back to her old life on the farm and never mixed outside. I don't think anybody around here had the faintest idea that she'd travelled the world. One year – it was 1974, I suppose – she went off for weeks on end. Robbie said to me: "Oh, she's gone off all over America and Canada. Wouldn't surprise me if she never came back." He said this with a laugh. Of course she did come back, and again she was almost unrecognizable from when she went. Had a new pair of glasses, looked just like an American. That was the last time she went away.

'From then on things started to get bad again. Robbie was seizing up. He just couldn't cope. He got a skin disease all over his arms and hands and legs – all over his feet too. It was agony for him to put on his boots. In the end he couldn't get into them at all. He came out to me in the yard in bedroom slippers, right through the mud. Then I heard he'd been to the doctor with depression and that he'd been ordered off work.

'So I had to cope on my own with Danovitz, and I wasn't too well myself either; I was often out of breath and had pains in my chest.

'Then one day Frances came out to talk to me in the shed. I could see she wasn't happy. "I don't know what to do about Robbie," she said. "He's no better and he's not getting any younger." "Have you had any luck finding someone for the farm?" I asked. "No," she said. "We'll have to sell up and find somewhere more modern. We can't go on like this. I've made up my mind."

'At first it seemed as if everything was going to be straight-forward. Robbie had a long talk with me. He said they were bent on going, but he wasn't sure when. They were going to look for a bungalow with a bit of garden. "You'll be all right," he said. "I dare say the new people will take you on." Frances seemed to do all the organizing. They would go off in the morning and they'd be out all day together looking at property. In the meantime Robbie seemed to lose interest in the farm. He just left us to get on with it. Alan was left very much in the background. I hardly saw him at all over the next year. He used to come out sometimes after dark and mooch around the sheds with a lantern, but you'd never see him during the day.

'The next thing I heard they'd found somewhere over in Crediton, a new place, and put a deposit on it. That's when Alan came into the picture and the rows started. It went on for months – from the summer of last year right through into the summer of this. There were terrible rows inside and out here in the yard with Alan making threats, and they weren't getting anywhere. You see, they needed Alan's permission to sell up, because he owned a portion of the farm himself. It was a mess. Anyway, in the end they went ahead without his permission in the spring; after all, Robbie owned the stock and the equipment and the barns were in his portion of the property. He put the farm on the market and people started turning up. At first Frances had seemed the strong one and taken the lead, but no sooner had they sold the stock than she started to get depressed. It had a lot to do with all the stuff in the house – when she started turning out drawers and deciding what to do with things. Once she came out with things to me. She said: "I think your wife might like this." It wasn't anything valuable – an old table spread or something like that. No sooner had I thanked her than she got fretful right there and then, and changed her mind. "Well, I'll see," she said. "I'll put it by for now." And she took it back into the house.

'The trouble was, the place they'd decided to buy was far too small to take all the stuff they had here, and yet she just couldn't bring herself to part with it. Then she started back on her old ways again, walking up to the churchyard at Brushford and over to Coldridge. I'd often see her when I went bell-ringing, wandering from grave to grave and scribbling notes.

'Apart from that they hardly went out. They stopped going to market and to Winkleigh; of course, out here there's a grocery van doing the rounds. But they didn't seem to eat at all. They began to look like skeletons. They never appeared, and if you caught sight of them by chance at the door they'd scuttle back in like rabbits in a burrow. I heard down at the village that they'd shaken hands on a deal with a farmer down in Essex or somewhere and were due to complete the sale on Michaelmas Day. But it was September and they'd decided nothing about their new home or getting rid of all the stuff they couldn't take. I think they'd changed their minds. They could easily have let the fields to neighbours on grazing agreements, but Robbie had shaken hands and to him that meant a binding agreement.

'At the beginning of September I met Frances in the lane. It was raining and she only had a thin summer dress on. I asked her if there was any news about the move and she just said: "We should have died here. We were born on the farm and we should die here." That's all she said and she kept saying it over and over again.

'A few days later I saw her from the high field at the back of the house. She was sitting on the garden seat looking out into the distance. I went on up to the fields at the back, and when I passed by later in the afternoon she was still there staring out as if she had all the time in the world.'

The Inquest

The inquest on the Luxtons' deaths was held in Okehampton Council offices on a melancholy day at the end of November. Winter was settling in and a cold mist shrouded the town. There were no immediate Luxton relatives, but the Shorts were there in strength and dressed in black. There was also a large number of journalists vying with each other for the attention of Detective Chief Superintendent Proven Sharpe, a huge-boned man with a great shock of silvery hair who moved with a posse of young detectives in close formation.

The unpleasant pathological details were dealt with swiftly, but there were two features that gave rise to some cross-questioning from the coroner, Colonel D. F. Brown.

Time of death is normally established by taking the rectal temperature of the body. It appeared that Frances's temperature was about the same as Alan's – even though circumstantial evidence indicated that she died some time after him. The Colonel also pursued the existence of some curious knife wounds on Robert's face that had been described by Horace William Barbow Kennard, the Home Office Pathologist:

'A number of vertical cuts were present on the cheeks and what appeared to be a cut with a blunt knife in front of the right ear. Two cuts were present, one below and one behind the right ear. These injuries were consistent with cuts produced by a blunt knife found in the dead man's pocket.'

Colonel: In regard to Robert Luxton, did you attach any importance to these wounds on his face and neck?

Kennard: They were consistent with wounds made with the

blunt pocket knife which was found in his pocket. In cases of suicide, it is surprising where they will make attempted cuts – in places where you and I would not think of making cuts. It is the thought of suicide.

Coroner: In regard to Alan Luxton, how do you account for the fact that parts of his brain were scattered very much further than in the case of Robert Luxton?

Kennard: It depends on how close the shotgun is placed to the forehead. In the farming community I have found they tend to favour the centre of the forehead where the humane cattle-killer goes. The weakest part of the head is at the forehead. I have known the brain to go 120 feet away from the body when the gun was held tight against the head. Therefore, in the case of Alan, the gun was held closer to the head than in Robert's case – and a great deal closer than Frances Luxton's case.

Coroner: But in the case of Robert and Alan, this was only inches away?

Kennard: Yes.

Coroner: Could you explain further as to the differences in temperature between the bodies?

Kennard: The difference in rectal temperatures between Robert and Alan was considerable – Robert's being a number of degrees higher. I would therefore say that Alan died first and Robert probably died one to two hours later. Frances Luxton had a rectal temperature almost the same as Alan, but was a slightly built female wearing only a nightdress and it was night-time. I would therefore expect her body to cool more rapidly than Alan's which was fully clothed. I therefore came to the conclusion that she had died after Alan but before Robert.

One of the principal witnesses was Fred Lyne, who stood up magnificently to the hushed and intense atmosphere of the courtroom, crowded out with policemen, solicitors, doctors and journalists. This was his statement:

'I have always regarded Robert as the Maister and took orders from him. He was always a reliable man, but Alan acted very strangely at times and for example walked around the farmyard in his pyjamas or with just a bag tied around his waist and nothing underneath. This happened on many occasions and the last time I saw him dressed like this must have been the Friday before the shooting. At times he struck me as being a bit mental but at other times was quite sensible and reasonable, although he was always shouting and swore very strongly at times. On such occasions I have heard Robert ordering him to get indoors out of the way.

'During May or June last, Robert mentioned they were going to sell the farm and that his brother was not very agreeable to it, and since then things were not very happy between them, and on occasions when working near the house I heard them arguing about it. Things appeared to come to a head about four months ago when someone had made a good offer for the farm, and I was having my lunch at about ten one morning when Frances came running out of the house crying and asked me to go into the house. She was very upset and knowing Robert was not very well I expected to see that something had happened to him. I followed Frances into the kitchen and she pointed towards Alan who was standing near the mantelpiece with a shotgun in his hands with the barrels pointed towards the floor. His face was very white and he looked wild. I did not feel sure what he was going to do but on looking at him I could see that he was in the right mind to do anything. Robert was standing near him and looked a bit worried. I looked at Alan and said, "What have you got there holding?" – meaning the gun, and could see that it was a double-barrelled shotgun with hammers. Alan said, "They

have had a good offer for the farm." I said, "That's good news."
Alan said, "What am I going to do?" I jokingly said there was
a field of hay that needs turning and that he was to go up the
garden or I would report him. He then immediately gave the
gun to Robert and I went out to the yard with Frances.
Frances said she and Robert were for leaving the farm but
Alan did not want to go. I said she should hide the gun and
take the cartridges out to the shed where I was having my
lunch. She brought them out and they stayed there for several
days, after which they disappeared, but I do not know where
they went or what happened to the gun. Frances mentioned
there were more cartridges in the house but she couldn't find
them. I last saw the Luxton brothers that afternoon.

'The next Tuesday I arrived for work at half past seven and
carried on working down near the cottage and at about ten
o'clock I saw a van go up towards the farm and return a few
minutes later at a fast speed. Shortly after eleven o'clock I was
taken by a policeman to the farm where I saw a body in the
farmyard which I identified as that of Alan.'

Danovitz did not give evidence, but his wife Janet Ann,
whom I had not met before, told of the events of the last few
days before the shooting. She worked at a poultry factory farm
and had helped Frances out with the housework occasionally:

'I have lived at Chub House for about twenty years; it is a
tied cottage owned by the Luxton family. On most Saturday
mornings I used to go to the farmhouse and help Frances
Luxton with the cleaning. In the kitchen there is a large beam
running across the ceiling and when I last cleaned the kitchen
about a fortnight before the tragedy a shotgun was hanging on
the side of the beam.

'The Thursday before the shootings I went up to the farm
and I saw the two brothers together in the yard. They were

arguing. The young brother was shouting at the older one. I heard him say, "You damned fool, you've sold the bloody farm and you've upset everyone." The younger brother then walked off. I did not hear anything else they said. Miss Luxton was in the house at the time; she didn't come out to them arguing.

'The younger brother Alan had a violent temper and appeared to be mentally unstable and I can't remember the last time he left the farm.

'Since July of this year it was a regular occurrence to hear the younger brother shouting or arguing about something. He was always arguing with the other two. At about two o'clock on the day before they died I went to the farmhouse to collect some milk but noticed nothing unusual. Frances came to the door, seemed all right in herself and let me have the milk I required. I never saw any of the family again.'

When Detective Chief Superintendent Proven Sharpe took the stand the courtroom was more than usually attentive. He was clearly a man who liked to question rather than be questioned, but he also relished the task of addressing an audience. With his commanding height, his swept-back silver hair and his ruddy countryman's complexion, he looked an ideal head of CID for Devon and Cornwall. Shotgun killings on lonely farms and unspeakable country matters were his stock-in-trade. For the first time he told the full and grisly details of the killings as they were viewed by the police, and in a policeman's inimitable language:

'When I arrived at West Chapple Farm I saw Detective Inspector K. Pinder and other police officers. Detective Inspector Pinder showed me the body of Alan Luxton which had a severe shotgun wound to the head and which was lying on the hard stone surface in the yard at the front of the farmhouse. There was a large pool of congealed blood which had not soaked into the ground around the head. The body was clad in pyjamas and boots which were unlaced. The presence of the pool of blood together with the distribution of the debris from inside the skull indicated that the fatal wound had been inflicted at the spot where the body was found.

'Apart from the absence of any firearm near the body, its position and the attendant circumstances were typical of those found in cases where persons have committed suicide by means of a self-inflicted shotgun wound to the head. In this connection, the presence of considerable powder-blackening around the bridge of the nose, suggesting that the muzzle of the weapon used had been held close to, if not in direct contact with, the forehead, together with the wooden stick lying across the right-hand side of the body and which Alan Luxton appeared to have been holding in his right hand, are most significant. The use of a stick to operate the trigger by a person committing suicide with a long-barrelled shotgun is quite common.

'After examining the scene where Alan Luxton's body was lying, I went with Detective Inspector Pinder to the garden at the back of the farmhouse where I saw the bodies of Robert Luxton and Frances Luxton. They both had severe shotgun wounds to the head and were lying close together. On the ground beside Robert Luxton's right leg was a double-barrelled shotgun. Also on the ground on the right-hand side of his body between the elbow and the hip was a short wooden stick. When the breech of the shotgun was subsequently opened it was found to contain a live cartridge and a spent cartridge. A live and a spent cartridge were also later found in Robert Luxton's trousers pocket. He was dressed in trousers, a vest, unlaced shoes and socks. The shotgun wound was very extensive indicating that it had been inflicted at close range and this, together with the weapon and stick lying beside the body and the actual position of the body, were indicative of the fatal wound having been self-inflicted. Although all the blood which had been discharged from the skull had obviously been quickly absorbed into the soft earth where Robert Luxton's body was lying, it was significant that the butt of the shotgun was fairly heavily stained with blood and it seemed that this blood-staining must have occurred elsewhere.

'Frances Luxton's body was clad in night attire. She was not wearing any form of footwear. The body was lying face downwards but partially inclined on the right side and it cannot be said that it was in a typical position which is found where a person has deliberately self-inflicted a fatal shotgun wound. In this case the injury to the head was also very extensive, which suggested that it must have been inflicted at very close range. Moreover, the original point of impact of the discharge from the weapon used appeared to have been the centre of the forehead. There was no evidence of a struggle having taken place, which does give rise to the possibility that Frances Luxton may not have resisted the person who inflicted the fatal wound.

'I examined the exterior of the farmhouse and noticed that a window into the dairy had been forced. I was informed by the officers present that this had been done by them when they first arrived at the scene to gain access into the farmhouse, as all the doors appeared to have been locked. When entry had been gained and the inside of these doors examined it was found that all the keys were in position in the locks on the inside. The first-floor window of Frances Luxton's bedroom facing out on to the back garden was open and swinging on its hinges, but there was no disturbance of the ground beneath the window to suggest that a person had left the premises by this means.

'There were four doors leading out of the farmhouse, two at the front and two at the rear, and in view of the suggestion that these doors had been locked with the keys on the inside when police first arrived at the scene I examined all the locks very carefully. In the case of the lock on the door leading from the kitchen into the back garden, I found that it was faulty and that on several occasions when turning the key into the locked position it did not activate the tongue. In addition there was also a latch on this door, the tongue of which was held in the closed position on the door jamb by means of a bent rusty nail. On occasions, when this latch was operated the door did not open. Because of these defects in the lock and catch of this door, the possibility of police officers carrying out a hurried check of the doors from the exterior and assuming that the door of the kitchen was locked (although this was not really the case) cannot be discounted.

'The inside of the farmhouse was generally in an untidy condition, but there was no evidence to suggest that there had been ransacking by an intruder who had unlawfully entered the premises. In cupboards and china cabinets of the downstairs rooms there were valuable pieces of silverware and other property which had not been disturbed. Upstairs in the bedroom which was obviously occupied by Alan and Robert Luxton, there was a locked safe, the key of which could be found without difficulty in the top drawer of a nearby chest. When the safe was opened there was nothing to suggest that the contents, which comprised nearly £1,000 in cash and other valuable securities, had been disturbed.

'I was joined at the farm later that day by Dr Kennard, Home Office Pathologist, and Mr Peter Prescott from the South Western Forensic Science Laboratory. They made more detailed examinations of the scenes and surrounding areas where the bodies were found.

'I arranged for a team of detective officers to make extensive inquiries amongst persons in the Winkleigh area and elsewhere who knew the deceased. As a result of these inquiries and the various statements taken, together with the examinations carried out at the farm, I came to the firm conclusion that a fourth person was not involved in the deaths of the deceased.

'On Wednesday 24th September I visited the farm again and, with Mr Prescott, examined the pool of congealed blood in the farmyard alongside which Alan Luxton's head had been lying. In this pool of blood we noticed what appeared to be the outline of the butt of a shotgun. When the butt of the shotgun found beside the body of Robert Luxton was superimposed over the outline in the pool of blood the two were found to coincide, indicating that this weapon had lain on the ground beside Alan Luxton's head after the fatal wound had been inflicted and adding some further weight to the theory that the injury was self-inflicted.

'Whilst it has not been possible from the police investigations to draw positive conclusions as to the sequence of events at the farm during the period when the three deceased died (apart from the fact that no fourth person was involved), it seems more than likely that Alan Luxton took his own life before his brother died and that the latter also committed suicide. As to when Frances Luxton met her death has been impossible to determine – that is, whether it occurred before her two brothers or at some time in between. In this connection, although it does not appear to have been self-inflicted, the possibility that she did not resist and could have acquiesced to the actions of the person who actually inflicted the fatal wound cannot be ignored.'

After Proven Sharpe's evidence the coroner asked him: 'In regard to the forked stick found beside the body of Robert Luxton – the end of the stick is towards his head rather than towards his feet. Is this normal?'

'This is not normal,' said Sharpe. 'The stick was used to operate the trigger but one cannot tell what will happen to the stick when the trigger is pulled when the stick is held in the hand.'

'This would explain the fact that the normal end of the stick was not used?' said Colonel Brown.

'Yes sir. When the stick is held in the hand, it does not matter which end is used.'

A solicitor representing the Luxtons then rose and asked: 'Inspector, you say you cannot rule out the possibility that Miss Frances Luxton did acquiesce in the shooting. Did I understand you to say that you could not absolutely rule out the possibility of suicide?'

'There are no factors to support suicide except that the shot-gun wound was inflicted at very short range,' said Sharpe.

'The body was in a reverse position to that which is normal,' went on the solicitor.

But Colonel Brown intervened snappily: 'This has all been covered already.'

'The wounds could not be self-inflicted?' insisted the solicitor.

'It would appear,' said Colonel Brown, 'that they could not be self-inflicted having regard to her position. She would find it difficult to shoot herself and then fall forward on all fours.'

'Suicide is extremely unlikely in view of her position,' added Sharpe.

'Were there any fingerprints on the guns?' the solicitor asked the policeman.

'No. Nothing, as the blood-staining had blurred them.'

In his summing up Colonel Brown suggested that Robert and Frances had heard a shot and rushed out to find the body of their brother. He went on: 'In their depressed state of mind, Robert could have shot his sister with or without her consent. If Alan had shot his sister, the gun would have been found by him, but it was not.

'There is strong evidence to suggest that the wounds received by Alan and Robert were both self-inflicted. In the case of Frances I think you can rule out the possibility of suicide. The evidence suggests she was killed by one or other of the brothers.'

At the end of a long afternoon of morbid police and forensic evidence, the jury retired to deliberate and the people in the court wandered out into the council office car park to smoke and stretch their legs. Detective Chief Superintendent Proven Sharpe indulged in some banter with the reporters.

We were called back after just fifteen minutes to hear a terse statement. Reading from a piece of paper Colonel Brown announced: 'In the case of the Luxtons we have reached the following verdict this afternoon, that Mr Alan Luxton committed suicide, and that Mr Robert Luxton first killed his sister and then himself committed suicide.'

There was an immediate hubbub in the courtroom, but there ended the legal process of the Luxton tragedy.

I returned to Winkleigh briefly the following March to attend the sale of the Luxtons' effects. I went down hoping that there would be some interesting personalia providing further clues about the Luxtons. The sale was held in the ugly community hall, the erection of which had divided the village in the thirties. The Luxtons' deaths had stirred up widespread interest in their belongings and crowds of people from far afield swarmed about the building before the sale began. There was something sacrilegious about the hard-eyed dealers and bustling housewives up-ending vases and candlesticks, pulling open drawers and scrutinizing cupboards.

I was particularly interested in a cardboard box containing several thousand postcards going back to the middle of the nineteenth century and a variety of books and Bibles, some of them annotated. The majority of the postcards were blank and

probably of little value, but there were some family photographs among them – one of them of Frances as a mild-eyed,
pretty young woman of nineteen or twenty. I wanted the lot
for that photograph alone.

The villainous-looking shotgun that had killed them was
also on sale, an old French piece with hammers, and it was
attracting considerable curiosity and excitement. The household goods spilled out into the backyard of the hall, and there
in the cold sunlight farming men with red hands and smoking
breath were rummaging among the rusty farm implements.

The sale started briskly at eleven o'clock. The streets of
Winkleigh were now jammed with vehicles and the hall was
crammed to capacity, with people sitting on window-sills and
every available surface. The bidding was aggressive and high.
The old deal kitchen table went for £175, the shotgun for
£160. There was a hushed atmosphere when the sale of
the engagement ring was announced. It was a two-stoned
diamond cross-over arrangement in an outmoded fifties-style
setting. It still sat in its original box. Behind me I heard
someone say, 'That's a doomed ring.' The bidding started at
£30 and soared rapidly to £155. It went to a dealer from
Plymouth. Dealers homed in on all the books and they went
for high figures – a set of Paley's *Evidences* fetched £150.

At last the box of postcards came up and I found myself
bidding against two other people in the hall; they dropped out
at £10. I took my box immediately, paid at the door and
walked up the village street to the King's Head for a drink.

Standing at the bar I fell into conversation with a woman I
at first took to be a farmer, but who turned out to be Susan
Barrett, a playwright and novelist, who had been researching
the Luxtons' story in the hope of writing a dramatic reconstruction for television. She told me that she was not altogether
sure she liked the Luxtons, and she had found West Chapple
distinctly creepy. She described to me her first visit:

'I wandered around for quite a long time and found it delightful. Then suddenly in that garden at the back, where Robbie and Frances killed themselves, the air seemed to go hot against my skin and there was a strange sort of pressure in the atmosphere. I turned and got out as fast as I could; it was like being hounded out by the pressure. I think that they killed themselves because there were no exits. They were down in a valley in awful solitude . . . the ways in and out are not obvious. To some people it could mean peace, tranquillity. To me it conveyed a sense of hopelessness – it's tempting like a cool pool on a hot day, but it's deep – you could drown in it.'

Before we parted she said: 'You know, I'm not sure that I can complete this project. Normally I'm a fairly robust person, but every time I've been over here to do some more research I've been sick in every lay-by between here and Taunton. My chief impression of Winkleigh has been of talking to people through a mist of nausea. It's got so bad that I'm wondering whether Frances Luxton is haunting me, making me ill to prevent my meddling in her affairs.'

Susan Barrett never did complete her project on the Luxtons, but eventually, in 1977, she very generously sent me forty pages of research notes including a treatment for a television play. In an accompanying letter she told me that she hoped the notes might be of use in the completion of my own book. She had decided to drop the idea of writing about the Luxtons, but she might, she said, incorporate some of the material in a novel about Mid-Devon.

In fact, I too had run into problems. The papers that William Luxton had given me were interesting, but useful only as background material. The key to the story really lay in my interviews, but these contained much repetitive and malicious gossip, particularly relating to the rumour that Frances and Robbie had been incestuous. There were also many stories about the Luxtons' meanness which I felt to be exaggerated. I was determined that I should be fair to the Luxtons, who now had no one to defend their reputations. More than once I was reminded of those plaintive lines copied out several times in Frances's hand:

> False witness did rise up
> They laid to my charge
> Things that I knew not
> They rewarded me evil for good
> To the great discomfort of my soul.

There seemed to me no way of constructing a fair and authentic account without a tedious series of provisos and disclaimers.

At length I was obliged to turn to other projects and the Luxtons' story lay neglected for several years, although never entirely forgotten.

West Chapple Revisited

Between 1976 and 1981 I occasionally met and corresponded with the Heath brothers, who kept me abreast of news from Winkleigh. In 1979 I learned with a pang of envy that a film crew had descended on West Chapple to make a film about the Luxtons called *The Recluse*. The director, Bob Bentley, and the cameramen had stayed at Headlands Manor Farm, and many of the locals had been used as extras, including the Heaths.

In the autumn of 1980 Derek Heath telephoned to say that they had seen a preview of the film in a pub in Hatherleigh. 'We didn't like it,' he said. 'It was much too dark and gloomy.' He was particularly put out by the fact that some crockery of his had been used in the kitchen scenes, but not displayed to any great advantage in the finished film.

Derek Heath eventually put me in touch with Bentley and in the summer of 1981 I was invited to see *The Recluse* in a private viewing theatre at the Twentieth Century Fox offices in Soho Square. The film told the story of the last day of the Luxtons' lives. It showed Robbie and Frances going to Hatherleigh to visit an estate agent, while Alan stayed at home haunted by the ghost of his father and episodes from his childhood.

The tale had a simple Wordsworthian quality. All the tensions between Robbie and Alan had been skilfully and economically drawn, and Bentley's interpretations seemed to me absolutely authentic. It lasted just half an hour and ended with a struggle between the two brothers over the shotgun. The final scene was of West Chapple viewed from high up on a neighbouring hill. The house is still and silent except for a dog barking. A door slams and a dim figure can be seen running from the back of the house across the orchard and out of sight. There is a long pause and then the sound of a single gunshot. The dog continues to bark.

It was an extraordinary experience to be sitting in a theatre in the heart of London watching on screen a place that had been so remote and secret both in reality and in my investigation. The film had been made entirely on location and all the interiors had been shot inside the farmhouse. Many of the furnishings had come from neighbouring Headlands Manor, and the Heaths and other old friends appeared as extras in Hatherleigh market place.

After the film we took a walk around Soho Square and talked about the 'tragedy'. He said that despite the three years he had spent making the film, he still did not know what it was about. He also admitted that the actors had felt a sense of trepidation about enacting those final scenes of the Luxtons' lives.

'It's become so much part of fiction that I've become detached from the reality of it,' he said. 'I became interested in the story when I read about it in the *Observer*. I was brought up in Bideford, North Devon, so it was of special interest to me. It was a year, though, before I went to my local library in London and looked up the press cutting. There was something in the story that had stuck with me. I wanted to make a film about it.

'On various visits to my parents in Bideford I took time to do some research and met John Gledhill, the present farmer on West Chapple Farm. I became more and more fascinated. I involved Paddy Fletcher, an old friend and colleague, to write the script with me. Together we eventually arrived at a screenplay that I used in the shooting of the film.

'We didn't set out to write about the problems of old people or farming life, although the film deals with these issues, but we tried to interpret the story in fictional terms as faithfully as we could.

'I had my reservations about what we were doing and so felt a terrible responsibility to the Luxtons to get it right and allow them through all the dramatic devices of the story and into the film. I still can't express what it is really about or what it has to say.'

I had gone to Bentley's film in trepidation. As the years passed I had felt increasingly guilty about not having completed a manuscript. Part of me hoped that his film would tell the Luxton story so successfully that I would at last be let off the hook. Another part of me was still possessive about the story, with a lingering hope that I would find a way of telling it myself. I greatly admired *The Recluse* and thought it a skilful reconstruction of the Luxtons' last hours, but the film raised far more questions than it answered. Bentley's Luxtons were not mine, and there was still a story to be told.

Then, just a week or two later, a copy of a new novel by Susan Barrett arrived in the post. It was called *The Beacon*. As I opened it, it crossed my mind that she had attempted what I had suspected for some time was the only feasible approach to the Luxtons' story – a fictional account.

In an accompanying note she referred me to a passage in the book that had been based on her first visit to West Chapple. 'It's interesting,' she wrote, 'how reality is transformed in fiction, but the passage is, I believe, an accurate evocation of what I saw and felt going up to the farmyard on that first day.'

I turned to page 46 and this is what I read:

The track was narrow. Untrimmed hazel and hawthorn, oak and beech reached out from the top of either hedge to meet overhead. Brambles caught at her skirt as she stepped to avoid deep ruts where dark water lay although there had been no rain. The sun had ceased to shine, and a heavy silence closed in on her. The track led on and down and round corners with such little indication of purpose that Kate considered turning back. But each corner that promised a view led her on, until after half a mile she turned a bend and saw the farmhouse lying below her in the hidden valley.

She stopped, to quieten her own noise – her fast breathing, and her mind. The farmhouse lay facing her – not peacefully slumbering as one might describe a picturesque thatched cottage, Kate thought, but dead. A horse would refuse to walk further; but I am human and therefore don't obey my instincts. I walk on, because after all I am only calling at a farm for cream. And birds are singing.

But birds are heartless; they sing through every human tragedy.

Kate walked on, down towards the farmhouse. The track ended at a gate leading into a large cobbled yard between two crumbling stone barns. Beside her, as she looked for the way to open the gate, corrugated iron blocked a gap in the hedge to her right.

Bright orange binder twine tied the broken-down gate and Kate spent some moments trying to undo it. Then she had trouble lifting the gate open wide enough to squeeze through without the gate falling over on top of her. Then she thought she'd better tie the gate shut again.

Kate crossed the yard, nettles growing through tangled bundles of wire netting, and – peeking big eyes and pricked ears from the hem of an old sack laid on a crate – three kittens. 'A kitten to take home?' thought Kate, feeling at once that she had been foolish, falsely sensing an atmosphere of gloom and evil where there was only a timeless placid rusticity.

The story, as it continued, bore no relation to the Luxtons at West Chapple. My remaining 'rival' had left me with a clear field and a conscience still burdened.

Eventually it was Proven Sharpe who acted as unintentional stimulus and led me back to West Chapple and the 'Luxton tragedy'. Sharpe had been unavailable for interview in 1975, but I wrote to him all the same telling him about my project and suggesting that he might at least be interested in talking about the problems of policing in remote rural districts. He never did reply to that letter.

Then one day in August of 1981 he telephoned to say that he had now retired and would like to meet for a chat.

We met at the Clarence Hotel opposite Exeter Cathedral and had lunch together. Robust and bustling, he had changed very little since I last saw him. He told me that he now worked for Securicor, mostly in Bristol, and kept himself extremely busy.

He seemed curiously reluctant at first to talk about the Luxtons, but approached the subject in a roundabout way. He wanted to tell me about a case that had particularly haunted him, one that he was proud to have 'cracked by determined and consistent detection work'. It was a striking story and I felt compelled to set it down later, as it became the prelude to my renewed interest in the Luxtons, Mid-Devon and all the people associated with the tragedy. This was Sharpe's story:

'Every Saturday night Paula, let's call her, used to go to a disco in Falmouth and walk home after it shut – that was normally at about 11.30. There was a bus used to leave Falmouth at about ten o'clock, and her parents were always on at her to catch it.

'On this particular night they'd been telling her to take the bus and not to walk. Anyway, she defied them and she didn't turn up at all. We found her the next day in a quiet country lane, sexually assaulted and battered to death with the granite boulders you find in the banks of the hedgerows around there. It was a particularly savage murder and it appeared to us that whoever had done it must have had unusual strength. The murderer had clawed into the bank in a frenzy, it seemed, and he'd held her to the ground with his foot. As well as her fatal injuries there were two footmarks on her stomach that had clearly come from crêpe soles because they were ribbed.

'We sent off photographs of the marks to a special shoe laboratory in Northampton and the results came back – yes, these were made by a specific kind of gym shoe commonly used in the Royal Navy.

'One of our first suspects was a man who lived on a secluded caravan site not far from the killing. He had been in various mental hospitals and had been involved in sexual assault in the past. He had been out at the time and had a terrible alibi that put him down as an obvious suspect. He had been out to a fish and chip shop and he could easily have met Paula on the way back.

'It was one of the worst interrogations I've ever conducted in my life. He just kept saying over and over again: "I didn't murder that girl!" I just couldn't get through to him. He certainly had the strength to do the crime; we made him do press-ups and he could do thirty without pausing, whereas the police officer looking after him could only do three! In the end everything centred on the shoes. This man only had one pair of shoes and they weren't ribbed gym shoes. So we had to let him go.

'We set up an investigation centre on the front at Falmouth and we interviewed certain categories of men. What you do is to put out an announcement for certain sorts of people to come forward. Now you know already who they all are and if any of them fail to turn up it shows they might have something to hide.

'Well, we asked all the senior boys at Falmouth Grammar School to come forward, and in each case we asked for alibis. They were all corroborated except one. He had a fairly good story, which was that he had been to a model railway club and had been there on his own. We were satisfied he hadn't got these crêpe shoes, but we put him under the microscope just the same, because by this stage we just weren't getting anywhere.

'Incidentally, we had sixteen people come forward to say that they had seen a man riding around the district on a bicycle at roughly the time when the disco had ended. The interesting thing was that none of them put the age of the cyclist under thirty, and one even said fifty.

'So here we were envisaging a man of middle age, with fantastic strength, possessing a pair of gym shoes – possibly attached to the Royal Navy. Needless to say we were putting the naval establishments under the microscope!

'Going back to the grammar school boy, who I shall call John, he said that he had a key to this model railway club which was situated in a Nissen hut at the back of the town's football ground. He said he'd been there with friends until ten o'clock and he left with them, but had decided to go back. He said he'd cycled off to get something to eat, then changed his mind and gone back because he discovered he had no money. Working on his models back at the club he said he lost all sense of time and that his watch had stopped at 10.15. When he eventually came out and looked at the time on the town clock it turned out to be 11.45.

'We interviewed everybody who might have had a sight of the club asking them if they remembered the lights being on or off. Eventually we found a man who had stayed behind at the football club bar to wash up glasses (well, we all know what that usually means). Anyway this man had gone out for a pee on to the football ground and he said exactly this: "I'm absolutely definite about the fact that the lights were out in the model railway club, because when they are on I turn myself away towards the town to pee, but when they are off I faces towards the Nissen hut."

'Once again we put this boy under the microscope and under interrogation he said, yes, he hadn't been in the club, in fact he'd been down on the derelict second station at Falmouth stealing a railway sign. We took him home and sure enough he had the sign; then we took him down to the railway station and asked him to show us how he'd taken down the sign. Well, the way he showed us he would have needed a pair of step-ladders. In fact, we learned later he'd originally got the sign with the help of friends.

'This time he confessed he'd been lying all along, and that he'd been frightened to admit what he'd really been doing which was cycling round the town looking for windows where he could see women getting undressed. Well, once he'd admitted this we knew it was him: here at last was the kinkiness. We went home with him and out came all his shoes and clothes. There wasn't a trace of blood on any of his clothes. We ripped his shoes to pieces and we put every millimetre under the microscope, and there it was – a definite trace of blood of the same group as the girl's. The boy's parents had been protecting him. The funny thing was they'd been too mean to destroy the shoes; they'd scrubbed them in the sink, but we found the trace of blood right under the uppers. After we confronted him with the crime he confessed.

'All well and good. But there was still the problem of the ribbed effect on the girl's stomach, because the boy's shoes were just ordinary plain soles. I spent hours pondering this problem, because although the boy had confessed I didn't want him changing his plea before I'd licked this particular problem. In the end I got a police girl to go through the exact motions of being pinned to the ground by a man with a foot on her stomach and I noticed that, in her attempts to resist, her stomach went into a concertina shape. Naturally the impression of the shoes would have been ribbed.'

Sharpe told his story with a curious compulsion and appeared greatly satisfied by having got it off his chest. He now seemed happy to talk about the Luxtons for a while, although he confessed that his memory was a little patchy about the details.

'The thing I'll never forget about the Luxtons was the problem we had with the flies. The bodies were completely fly-blown and some of the coppers simply couldn't stand it. We had to use masses of spray on them to get near the bodies.

'Police work is never quite straightforward in a place like Winkleigh. You have to adopt a different attitude in the depths of the country. When it comes to crime it's often a case of being more lenient. An old lady who steals a half-pound of butter in a place like Winkleigh is known to everyone. The whispering starts and they make her life hell. She's ostracized and treated like a pariah. She's punished for the rest of her life. By the same token it's extremely difficult to get things out of people in communities like Winkleigh; you've got to be very devious and patient. They can clam right up. On the other hand, you can get a lot of vindictive stories about individuals that are misleading. In the case of Winkleigh they all had it in for Alan, the youngest brother, because he'd had a history of mental illness and was rather strange. They were determined that it was Alan who had murdered his brother and sister, then done himself in. Whereas the story turned out to be quite different. We talked with dozens of people in the locality, and if we'd just taken notice of them the verdict at the inquest might have pointed to him as a murderer. Like the case of Paula, it always comes back to long, hard detection work.

'There were lots of letters from all over England about the Luxton case. We were pestered by some character in Portsmouth, I think it was, who had seen it all occur in a dream. But I was very struck by it and, I must say, developed a theory of my own. Of course, my guess is as good as yours, but I think what happened was that Robert was absolutely torn: he'd shaken hands on a deal and then changed his mind. Country folk are like this. A shake of the hand is more important than signatures on a contract.

'I think that Robbie Luxton had had too much time to mull over it. I dare say that the other chap, the youngest brother, shot himself without any difficulties because he was fairly crazy already. But with Robert it was a question of terrible conflict. How else could you murder your own sister and do yourself in?'

My meeting with Sharpe, so soon after Bentley's film and Susan Barrett's book, rekindled my interest and my determination to do something at last with the Luxton story, even if it was simply to describe my quest.

That same afternoon I attempted to track down the medical file on Alan Luxton at the Wonford Hospital, where all records for mental patients in the county of Devon have been centralized. I had no success, but before I left one of the members of the psychiatric staff came up and told me that he had been particularly interested in the Luxtons and had followed the case closely. For many years, he said, he had specialized in the occurrence of stress and mental illness in rural occupations, and he had treated many patients from the Mid-Devon area. As we walked through the grounds of the Wonford Hospital he delivered a brief and enlightening lecture.

'Living in the remote countryside does not offer immunity to mental illness. It strikes right across the board: town, country, suburbs . . . every nationality and culture. I dare say the Russians fix their figures to indicate they're less mad than everybody else, but it's the same East and West. There's only one community I know of which seems to have a lower incidence of schizophrenia than the average – that's the Huttites in North America. Nevertheless, in an enclosed community one wonders how much their very seclusion alters the statistics. Mid-Devon is a case in point. It's a weird place where people can hide, where people can behave in an abnormal fashion without discovery. A person indulging in bizarre behaviour patterns in Mid-Devon is less likely to be referred to medical investigation than someone in Exeter.

'I know of a couple in Mid-Devon – they lived somewhere off the Exeter-to-Bideford road: the husband used to ride a bicycle and pull his wife along by the neck with a rope. He'd cycle down to the village like this right in the middle of the road. The locals had grown used to it and wouldn't have dreamt of trying to restrain him. They lived in a caravan in a remote field and didn't bother anybody; they were allowed to carry on. If it had happened here he would have been put on a Section 29 – a compulsory treatment order.

'In places like Mid-Devon you find that it's not the maddest members of the family who end up in hospital but the weakest: what I'm saying is that the whole family may be mad, but it's often the weakest physically who breaks down under the strain of the other members of the household. This might very well have been the case with Alan, who was said to have been fairly normal in his youth. Heaven knows what misery and torment he might have been put through by his elder brother and sister, and indeed his own mother and father. Who knows what goes on in a family cut off from normal social contact?

'I remember a husband from Mid-Devon on one of my wards. He was a hard-working farmer and came in with a breakdown; he was in very low spirits and depressed. When visitors' day came around his wife and his teenage son turned up on the ward. She was like something out of a comic opera and it was immediately apparent to me – as it clearly hadn't been to her own country doctor – that she was schizophrenic, and so was the son. The son, who was about seventeen, seemed to think he was a kangaroo or something. He kept leaping all over the ward with his fingers in his ears.

'I would say, though, that the Luxtons were a typical example of a depressive state working its way through a whole family. It reminds me very much of a case I came across recently – and these cases are on the increase – where a man and wife killed their children and themselves because they were convinced that the nuclear holocaust was imminent. They were overcome by an appalling sense of futility and hopelessness – absolutely nothing left to live for, no future. This is quite different from those sudden inexplicable acts, or those cases where the patient has been obsessed with the *idea* of suicide for a long period of time. Suicide in schizophrenics is quite different again. The primary delusions in a schizo-phrenic are typically those of a man who feels that he is being controlled by an outside force, like a puppet on a string. He will construct all sorts of theories around his delusion, such as cosmic rays, outside forces of all kinds; in your wildest dreams you couldn't come anywhere near their sort of experience.

'The depressive, on the other hand, is compelled much more by considerations that we can all appreciate. I must say that in the case of the Luxtons, I'm puzzled. I'm convinced that Robbie was suffering mainly from depression, and normally a depressive in his state doesn't have the energy to kill anybody but himself. He's totally engrossed in his own state. I suppose it's just possible that Frances begged him to kill her, made it easy for him. There was certainly not the slightest evidence of a struggle. She could have saved herself by just walking away from him.

'I can only speculate that the Luxton case is one where the familial ties were so strong that life became unthinkable after the first brother had killed himself. He, of course, seems to have contemplated suicide over a long period. There would have been strong identity with him, anxiety about the con-sequences, the fear of outsiders coming in, the sense of guilt;

and all this coming on top of the trauma of the previous
months.

'They were extremely close, this family. The tragic depar-
ture of one would have precipitated a hysterical episode in
which they worked up enough courage to follow suit. That's
where the cuts on Robbie's face came in. He could well have
stood before the mirror making those cuts while stoking up
courage towards the end. Moral considerations like Christi-
anity would have counted for absolutely nothing at a time
like this. Their emotions would have been in a state of shock
and all normal moral reasoning completely suspended. A
depressed person always ends it on the strength of emotion
rather than the force of intellect.

'The pity about the Luxtons is that they seemed to have
nobody they could turn to. I don't think that their problems
were excessive. It was reported in the press that they left about
£350,000, all of which went to the Church through the wills
of Robert and Frances. Alan was intestate so his money passed
into their estates. With that sort of money they could have
made a pretty painless transition into retirement. But again
it was that peculiar locality, those hidden valleys and high
hedges, the secretiveness. They're a people with a difference
... they're Mid-Devonians.'

As we shook hands, he said, 'You really should read Emile
Durkheim on suicide. You might find it enlightening.'

Later that afternoon I wandered into the general section
of the main library in Exeter and took out Durkheim's *Suicide*
from the open shelves. I found nothing on suicide pacts, but
there was one whole chapter entitled 'Imitation'. He wrote
this:

The idea of suicide may undoubtedly be communicated by
contagion. In 1813 in the little village of Saint-Pierre-Monjau, a
woman hanged herself from a tree and several others did likewise

at a little distance away. Pinel tells of a priest's hanging himself in the neighbourhood of Étampes; some days later two others killed themselves and several laymen imitated them. When Lord Castlereagh threw himself into Vesuvius, several of his companions followed his example.

The last case rather puzzled me, for I had been under the impression that Castlereagh had slit his throat with a penknife in the comfort of his home in England.

I skimmed on, but could find no explanation that seemed to apply to the case of the Luxtons. At length I came upon a passage that seemed to shed some light at least on the curious paradox that an ancient family threatened with extinction should choose to hasten its own end:

It has sometimes been said that because of his psychological constitution, man cannot live without some attachment to some object which transcends and survives him, and the reason for this necessity is a need we must have not to perish entirely. Life is said to be intolerable unless some reason for existing is involved, some purpose justifying life's trials. When, therefore, we have no other object than ourselves we cannot bear the thought that our efforts will finally end in nothingness, since we ourselves disappear. But Annihilation terrifies us. Under these conditions one would lose courage to live, that is, to act and struggle, since nothing will remain of our exertions.

I shut the book and went out to have tea in a cafeteria overlooking Exeter Cathedral. About me on all sides were happy-looking old ladies in fine hats. Annihilation held little terror for them, it seemed, as they tucked enthusiastically into mountains of Devon cream cakes.

The next day I went out to West Chapple. As I drove down the lane to the farmhouse I noticed new posts and barbed wire and I could see the gleaming corrugated roofs of new sheds behind the old Round House barn. There was brightly painted machinery and stacks of breeze blocks; there was a businesslike atmosphere of progress and prosperity. The farm-house was transformed: the thatched half had been slated and the walls freshly painted.

I came upon John Gledhill at the back of the house digging a trench across the lawn for a new drain. He was a wiry young man, slightly round-shouldered, as if with the drudgery of farmwork. He looked at me directly with dark, fierce eyes and invited me into the house for a cup of tea. The kitchen had been repainted and there was a new pine table and a royal blue Raeburn stove with bright copper piping leading up to the ceiling. The reception rooms were now tastefully furnished and fitted with pastel-coloured carpets. The freshly papered walls were hung with eighteenth-century paintings of ships and prize cattle. Upstairs there was a smart bathroom, and the bedrooms were light, airy and cheerful.

Back in the kitchen with a mug of steaming tea in his hand he told me he had made a bit of money out in Canada and had bought West Chapple with a hefty mortgage. 'I'm glad somebody's going to write about the farm,' he said. 'I don't mind telling you, I've become rather obsessed with the Luxtons. Paul Danovitz works for me now; Fred Lyne never came to visit the farm again after I moved in – I suppose he must have felt rather bitter. Anyway, Paul and I are always talking about the Luxtons: we'll be working up in a field, then Paul will suddenly remember something Robbie said, or the way he did things, and he'll imitate him – a rather high-pitched voice and a gesture of the hand on the cheek as if brushing away a fly.

'I inherited a model farm in some ways; it had been lovingly cared for in the past and they knew what they were doing; they certainly knew more about real farming than a lot of the people around here. But they were old-fashioned; they just let it tick over in the business sense, not spending a single penny. Well, you've got to be tight to make money out of farming. They weren't trying to increase and expand. They were just standing still. Mind you, they were putting back everything they were taking out. Of course, this is a beautiful farm – all the fields face south which means that they've got thirty per cent more grass than their neighbours with fields facing north.

'They had a flock of about one hundred and fifty ewes; they were all Long-wools. That's tradition for you. That goes back to the days when you reckoned to get a sizeable return on the sheep's wool. Nowadays a farmer is thinking solely of the butcher. Anyway, I'm keeping a flock of four hundred ewes on exactly the same acreage. I would think I have proportionately more cattle, too. Mind you, I don't keep horses or cows. At the moment I'm getting two and a half times more crop yield and that's going up all the time. But it's a different sort of farm now. You won't see vast changes just walking round, but I'm re-seeding regularly, a thing they never did, and I'm fertilizing by helicopter and crop spraying. In fact, I use every modern trick in the book. Can you believe it, they used to pick the dock leaves by hand!

'But I'm not sure that I'm actually better off than the Luxtons. My turnover is immeasurably better than theirs, but I've got to keep going to the bank. You can think of it in terms of sheep. How many sheep does it cost to buy a modern tractor? Well, it will cost five hundred. The Luxtons managed without a tractor; I can't. And I have to produce four sheep a week to pay for Paul's wages. The way the Luxtons did it, payment in kind – for wood, milk, eggs, accommodation and everything – it was more like one sheep a week. And that was no more than it was costing their grandfather for a farm labourer. A lot of people round here think the Luxtons were mean; I can think of a lot who are meaner. It was all in order to survive.

'Take the woods. There are a lot of woods on this farm and they looked after them. Robbie always believed that wood might become valuable again one day, that it would "come back". He thought as much of wood as he did of money; every stick was counted and he sold it and made money out of it. All their heating was done with wood and he paid people with wood. Paul and I are still burning Luxton wood that was stored seven or eight years ago.

'Of course, the tightness became an obsession. Paul tells an appalling story – how Robbie made him turn out his pockets after threshing on that old Victorian thing in the barn. You see, Paul had got hold of some of his own poultry one year, and Robbie was determined that they weren't going to be fed at his expense, with his corn. But when you think about it, when you think back over the several generations of struggle to survive you can understand it. I know it's a bit of a cliché, but farming to the Luxtons was a way of life, whereas to me it's a business. I'll give you an example. I've opened up wells in several places on the farm so that I can water my flocks and herds where they are and cut down on movement and labour. The Luxtons could have done the same, but they chose to bring every animal down into the yard for water twice a day. This meant a hell of a lot of work, but it gave them the opportunity to inspect every animal and to prevent problems before they developed.

'Most of Paul's stories about the Luxtons are unflattering, but he still regards them with an odd affection. They didn't treat poor Paul very well, I'm afraid. There's a bit of history there, I suppose. He was a Tot worker, a Russian who had gone over to the Germans and was then released by the Allies, and I dare say they regarded him as a sort of prisoner of war. You know the Tot workers used to do all the dirty jobs around the country. Paul didn't have any friends except the Ukrainians who came over to Huddersfield with him. I suppose he had to be careful, to be grateful. He never complained.

It's rather sad, you know. Recently he asked me if he could go and visit his Ukrainian friends in Huddersfield. I asked him if he needed any money and he said he wouldn't need any. "No," he said. "Things are very cheap up in Huddersfield." I made him take a five-pound note because I knew he would be in trouble. Off he went to Huddersfield. The next day I was out in the yard, and suddenly there was Paul standing next to me. He'd been to Huddersfield, spent his five pounds within ten minutes, and then found that all his friends were dead or gone. So he came straight back. For years he'd been talking about his friends in Huddersfield as if they were a thriving, vital little community, as if nothing had ever changed. God knows what he'll talk about now.

'It doesn't much bother me living in a house where there has been a violent tragedy.'

He told me that he came from a family which had had experience of suicide.

'You see, in our family we simply pack it in when we can't face tomorrow's laughter, never mind tomorrow's misery; when we feel we've had enough.

'When I first came to the farm I thought it was beautiful but I found it absolutely dead. I suppose I was spooked in that sense. Most farms are alive; but something had gone out of West Chapple. I went into the building where they had the cider press and I nearly jumped out of my skin at the sight of a jacket and cap hanging on a nail in the twilight; I suppose they must have been Robbie's. But what really did me was finding the shed with the water-wheel; it completely terrified me. It had something to do with the depth of the wheel. I felt a terrible pressure and I had to get out. I thought I could never live in that place. I stayed awake all night and by morning I got over it. I've put a strand of barbed wire across the entrance now.'

After a pause, he said: 'There's only been one strange event since I came here. One morning I looked through the kitchen window and saw a short, stocky figure in work clothes standing in the yard. By the time I got to the door he had completely vanished.

'It's interesting how suddenly suicides can happen. There was a shotgun suicide outside here just the other day. It was a young farmworker. He scraped a car as he was passing in his van. The other people weren't terribly hurt or anything, but I think there was a bit of blood on one of the passengers' faces. He went over to look at them, peered into the car at them, then he strolled back to his van, got a shotgun and blew his head off.

'Then there was the case of Cecil Ash who used to work over at Westacott. One day he went down to the New Inn at Sampford Courtney with a shotgun. He went to the little window where they do off-sales and asked for the governor. The landlord was playing darts at the time; he strolled over and poked his head through the window and Ash blasted him into eternity. Then he went back to Westacott and blew his own head off in the yard over there. Then people remembered that he'd been going around for weeks complaining that the governor at the New Inn had been "talking about him".

'I'm not really from these parts; I come from Wiltshire, so I'm an outsider. You've got to understand that farmers around here don't really farm.

'Most of these people have other business interests – bed and breakfast and all that; one of them is even a poet – probably makes more out of poetry than farming. But *real* farming is no fun; you either have to live like the Luxtons and be tight as hell – which *is* hell – or go for high productivity. But it's risky. Farming is like a great money-sucking machine: it sucks you in at one end and spits you out at the other, penniless. Most people are "farming to leave", as they say around here – putting nothing back in, spending nothing; farmers do that when they've decided to sell up. They just take, take, take out of the land and put nothing back.'

That afternoon Gledhill and I walked back down the lane together. He had kept the old Victorian machinery and claimed that he could probably get it working if necessary. But the old methods had completely given way to the new. A smart-looking combine was parked by the new barns and Danovitz chugged contentedly past on a tractor. Electric fencing and fertilizer bags were everywhere in evidence and Gledhill entertained me with his plans to produce lambs using factory-farming methods. Opposite Chub House there were builders busily at work with cement-mixers in the Round House barn.

Several weeks later John Gledhill threw a party at West Chapple to celebrate the refurbishing of the old Round House barn as a cottage. There were hundreds of cars parked along the track up to the farmhouse and a huge bonfire had been made of the last remnants of the Luxtons' firewood, so carefully conserved over the generations. There were coloured lights and lanterns, a barbecue and disco dancing. The Heaths were there, and a trendy vicar; so were Mrs Ennismore and her husband. There were dozens of the Winkleigh acquaintances I had made in the course of my investigation. There were farmworkers and butchers, policemen and nurses, writers and artists. Some of us were strangers to Winkleigh with little or no farming tradition, no abiding links with the Mid-Devon soil. Others had been there through their ancestors since time immemorial.

We completely took possession of the place. We jived and rocked and drank in the farmyard and in the garden; we laughed and yelled in the barns and the outhouses. West Chapple had never seen anything like it and any lingering Luxton shade had surely fled by dawn.

Only time will tell.

FOR THE BEST IN PAPERBACKS, LOOK FOR THE

In every corner of the world, on every subject under the sun, Penguin represents quality and variety – the very best in publishing today.

For complete information about books available from Penguin – including Pelicans, Puffins, Peregrines and Penguin Classics – and how to order them, write to us at the appropriate address below. Please note that for copyright reasons the selection of books varies from country to country.

In the United Kingdom: For a complete list of books available from Penguin in the U.K., please write to *Dept E.P., Penguin Books Ltd, Harmondsworth, Middlesex, UB7 0DA*

In the United States: For a complete list of books available from Penguin in the U.S., please write to *Dept BA, Penguin, 299 Murray Hill Parkway, East Rutherford, New Jersey 07073*

In Canada: For a complete list of books available from Penguin in Canada, please write to *Penguin Books Canada Ltd, 2801 John Street, Markham, Ontario L3R 1B4*

In Australia: For a complete list of books available from Penguin in Australia, please write to the *Marketing Department, Penguin Books Australia Ltd, P.O. Box 257, Ringwood, Victoria 3134*

In New Zealand: For a complete list of books available from Penguin in New Zealand, please write to the *Marketing Department, Penguin Books (NZ) Ltd, Private Bag, Takapuna, Auckland 9*

In India: For a complete list of books available from Penguin, please write to *Penguin Overseas Ltd, 706 Eros Apartments, 56 Nehru Place, New Delhi, 110019*

In Holland: For a complete list of books available from Penguin in Holland, please write to *Penguin Books Nederland B.V., Postbus 195, NL–1380AD Weesp, Netherlands*

In Germany: For a complete list of books available from Penguin, please write to *Penguin Books Ltd, Friedrichstrasse 10 – 12, D–6000 Frankfurt Main 1, Federal Republic of Germany*

In Spain: For a complete list of books available from Penguin in Spain, please write to *Longman Penguin España, Calle San Nicolas 15, E–28013 Madrid, Spain*